THE MYSTERY OF
MONASTERY FARM

H. R. NAYLOR

1st WORLD
LIBRARY
Literary Society

The Mystery of Monastery Farm

H. R. Naylor

© 1st World Library, 2006
PO Box 2211
Fairfield, IA 52556
www.1stworldlibrary.com
First Edition

LCCN: 2006907705

Softcover ISBN: 1-4218-2426-4
Hardcover ISBN: 1-4218-2326-8
eBook ISBN: 1-4218-2526-0

Purchase *"The Mystery of Monastery Farm"*
as a traditional bound book at:
www.1stWorldLibrary.com/purchase.asp?ISBN=1-4218-2426-4

1st World Library is a literary, educational organization
dedicated to:

- Creating a free internet library of downloadable ebooks

  - Hosting writing competitions and offering book
    publishing scholarships.

1st World Library Literary Society

Giving Back to the World

"If you want to work on the core problem, it's early school literacy."
- James Barksdale, former CEO of Netscape

"No skill is more crucial to the future of a child, or to a democratic and prosperous society, than literacy."

- Los Angeles Times

Literacy... means far more than learning how to read and write... The aim is to transmit... knowledge and promote social participation."
- UNESCO

"Literacy is not a luxury, it is a right and a responsibility. If our world is to meet the challenges of the twenty-first century we must harness the energy and creativity of all our citizens."

- President Bill Clinton

"Parents should be encouraged to read to their children, and teachers should be equipped with all available techniques for teaching literacy, so the varying needs and capacities of individual kids can be taken into account."
- Hugh Mackay

CHAPTER I

A GREAT BANK ROBBERY

On the eleventh day of April, 18 -, the officers of the Bank of England were greatly excited on receiving notice of a special meeting called for that night at ten o'clock, an unusual hour, and indicating, surely, something of great importance. Promptly at the hour appointed fifteen directors occupied their usual places in the council chamber. There were also present two paying tellers, which was not usual. Besides these two bank clerks was observed Major Andrews, the well-known chief of the Bow Street detective service, and by his side sat two of his assistants. As yet, there were only five persons present who knew the cause of this meeting - the president, cashier, and the chief and his assistants.

No time was permitted to waste. The president of the bank in a few nervous words asked the cashier to state the object of the call. Mr. Bone at once stated that there were strong indications that a robbery of the bank had been perpetrated; that a large amount of currency had been abstracted from the paying teller's room. Hence this sudden call for consultation; this, also, accounted for the unusual presence of Chief Andrews and his colleagues. He then called on Mr. Roe, the senior paying teller, to make a statement of what he knew of the matter.

Mr. Roe arose, and told that at nine o'clock that morning in his preparations for business he had brought from the vault a quantity of currency and placed it with other moneys on a side table conveniently situate for ready use. And that when, about two o'clock, he had occasion for its use, it was gone. Everything possible had been done to gain a clue, but there was not the slightest thing upon which to hang the faintest suspicion.

Major Andrews, stepping in front of the table, then requested permission to ask Mr. Roe a few questions simply for information. This permission was at once granted.

"Mr. Roe," asked the chief, "what was the general appearance of this money? Was it loose or in a package?"

"It was a neat package," replied Mr. Roe, "wrapped in brown paper, with its character and value marked distinctly on the wrapper."

"You say," said the chief, "'character and value distinctly marked on the wrapper.' Please to explain what you mean by these terms."

"I mean," replied the teller, "by 'character' that there were one hundred and fifty one-thousand-pound notes, and by 'value' the value of the package - one hundred and fifty thousand pounds."

"Mr. Roe," continued the major, "is it the custom of your department to have so large an amount of currency upon your side table?"

"No, sir," replied the teller, "but I had been notified that a large draft would be presented today, and this package came nearest to the amount spoken of; consequently, I selected and brought it to my table out of the vault to be in readiness to pay the draft when presented."

"You say you had been notified that a large draft would be presented. May I ask who notified you?"

"The cashier told me this morning when we were getting ready to open," was the prompt reply.

"Mr. Roe, when did you last see this money?"

"This morning about a quarter after nine, when it was placed upon my table; I counted the notes."

"Mr. Roe, do you feel free to tell the Board the name of the party who was expected to draw on you for this large amount?"

The teller's head dropped somewhat, and after a slight hesitation he replied: "Major, I cannot do this in accordance with the rules of the bank."

"Ah! that is all right, Mr. Roe; I forgot your rules. We can get at this in some other way. Mr. Roe, will you tell us if you did cash the large draft today which you say the cashier had indicated?"

"Yes, sir. I cashed a draft for one hundred and thirty-eight thousand pounds."

"Mr. Roe, was anyone in your room during banking hours?"

"Yes, the president and cashier both visited my room; it is their custom and, I believe, duty to do so each day."

"When did you first miss the package?"

"When the large draft was presented about two o'clock."

"What did you do then?"

"I spoke through the 'phone to Mr. Bone, asking him to come in."

"Does not the porter come to your room occasionally?"

"He never comes into the room after nine o'clock."

"Cannot other clerks enter?"

"Not without permission. The door fastens with a spring lock."

"How about your lunch?"

"Our lunch is handed us at half-past twelve through the door which we open."

"Now, Mr. Roe, with your knowledge of the case, what is your conviction concerning this lost package of money?"

"Major, I am compelled to say that I have not the faintest suspicion as to how it was taken."

Moving suddenly around, the major looked at the cashier and said: "Mr. Bone, what was your business in the teller's room this morning?"

"It is one of my duties, morning and evening, to tally the cash taken from the vault and returned in the evening."

"How long were you there this morning?"

"Perhaps fifteen or twenty minutes."

"When were you there the next time?"

"About half-past two, when Mr. Roe 'phoned me to come to his room, and I again opened the vault, that the teller might get some money to cash the large draft of one hundred and thirty-eight thousand pounds."

Much discussion followed this informal catechising, but the only thing evident was that the package was lost. How it had disappeared, or where it was, none could so much as guess.

Here were twenty men - thorough business men - several of whom had had large and successful banking experience, among them a cashier than whom there was no brighter financier in the great city of London, and the chief of a peerless detective force, with two of his shrewdest colleagues. All were nonplussed, annoyed, humiliated, returning to their homes and leaving the great building in charge of half a score of sturdy watchmen, safer, it would seem, in the night than in the day.

Next day several city newspapers had the following:

"REWARD

"A reward of TEN THOUSAND POUNDS will be paid for the arrest of the party or parties who abstracted a valuable package of Bank of England notes April 11, 18 -, from said bank. This currency can be of no value to the thieves, as the bank holds a list of the numbers, and their circulation has been ordered stopped. The receiver of any of these notes will be liable to arrest."

Nearly every important newspaper in the kingdom copied this item. Besides this, a list of the numbers of the lost notes was sent to every banking institution in England and America.

CHAPTER II

MONASTERY FARM

Billy Sparrow stood leaning against the gate post, looking down upon the river three hundred yards away. He and his two helpers had been cultivating corn and tobacco through a long June day; and now the sun was going down, and he was making his plans for tomorrow's work. Billy had just closed his fourth year as master of Monastery Farm. Billy was an Englishman from Durham County, having attended school in Barnard's Castle three years, with an additional two and a half years spent at the agricultural college in Darlington. He then married the girl of his choice and for four years superintended his father's farm; then, with their one child, three years old, set sail for America to seek his fortune, and four weeks later landed in New York.

Billy had letters of recommendation from the Wesleyan minister, Dr. Walsh, his father's physician, and old Squire Horner. But in vain did Billy present these credentials as he tramped the streets - nobody seemed to need his services in a city containing millions of people. Billy's capital was getting low and he was becoming discouraged. From one of those profitless tramps he was returning one evening when he observed the word "parsonage" on a door plate. He had always had a friend in a preacher in his native town; why not make the acquaintance of this one? Perhaps he might tell him of some sort of employment. Without stopping to think further he pulled the bell. In a moment or two he found himself in the presence of a young man, one but little older than himself, and the stranger was invited inside, feeling very much at home with the preacher.

After quite a lengthy conversation the preacher remarked: "You are a farmer; New York is no place for you. I would advise you to go out into the country; and, by the way, I believe I saw, a day or two since, an advertisement for a man to take charge of a farm."

After some search on the part of the minister the paper containing the announcement was found. Billy, having eagerly read the advertisement, thanked the minister, pushed the paper into his pocket, and speedily left the house. He returned to the humble apartment that he had secured, and as the little family partook of their frugal evening meal, his wife Nancy, addressing her husband, said: "I think we had better get out of this expensive city, somewhere into the country, where it is cheaper living, and where you may find something to do more to your liking."

"Well, Nancy," replied Billy, "this is the second time today that this advice has been given me, for," he added, pulling the newspaper from his pocket, "a minister gave me a paper in which there is an advertisement for a farmer, and advised me to look into it. Here it is," and he read as follows:

> "WANTED - A FARMER. Wanted, competent man, not afraid of work, to take charge of a farm of two hundred acres in - County, New York. A good house to live in, and good wages to the right man. References required. Apply by mail or in person to J. M. Quintin, Centerville Landing, -
>
> County, New York."

"Why," exclaimed Nancy, "I believe that is providential."

After pondering the subject awhile Billy wrote to Mr. Quintin, enclosing his credentials, and mailed the letter immediately.

In less than a week he received the following reply:

"William Sparrow, Esq., New York.

"I have just received your application for the position on Monastery Farm in answer to my advertisement. In replying I want to be candid with you. In a word, unless you are an expert farmer your application cannot be considered. If, therefore, you have any doubts about being able to meet the requirements, there is no need for further correspondence. This is a first-class farm and must be worked by first-class methods. The opening is an especially good one for the right man. Perhaps you had better come up and see the place, and give us a chance to see you. Come by boat to Centerville Landing. Let me know the time of your arrival, should you decide to come, and someone will meet you.

"J.W. QUINTIN, Trustee."

Billy read this letter with somewhat mixed feelings. There was no mistaking its meaning. This man spoke out. Its very brusqueness disconcerted the unsophisticated young man. His experience was quite limited. He had managed his father's one-hundred-acre farm several years, and it had paid very well. But he had always had his father's advice; of which he would be deprived in this his greater work. He read the letter to Nancy, and she was similarly impressed.

Finally Billy remarked: "I will find the preacher and ask his advice," and without further words he started to Washington Square, where his newly-found friend lived.

He was ushered into the library. He had never seen so many books before in one place. While he was glancing around in his surprise, the preacher entered. "Good evening, Mr. Sparrow," he said. "How are you? Have you found any employment yet?"

Billy handed him the letter which had brought him there, saying: "I received this letter today, and, if you please, I should like to have your advice about it."

The preacher opened the letter, and as he did so gave a little start. Then he smiled as he glanced down at the signature. He finished reading with a decidedly happy expression on his face, and Billy asked: "Can you tell me about this place, and of the man?"

"O, yes," was the ready reply, "I know both the place and the man; the fact is, that is my county, and Quintin is my friend. I never had a better friend than Jerry Quintin. I always spend my vacation there. I lived there from the time I was ten years old until I was twenty-three, and always go there in summer-time for a few weeks' rest - occupying my old room, eating with the boys, and roaming in the woods; I know every tree and bypath; yes, and many a swim have I had in the old river. Jerry Quintin," he continued, "as we used to call him. Why, I've known him since I was a child. Do you want to hear about him? Well, when he was a youth, not quite out of his teens, Mr. Thorndyke gave the land on which the Monastery stands, Quintin was made chairman of the board of trustees, and treasurer also. He has handled every dollar of the funds, superintended the erection of all the buildings, the laying off of the Monastery Park, and had charge of the farm; and through all the years no auditing committee had ever found an inaccuracy in his accounts. Foresight, sagacity, rectitude are synonymous terms with the name of Quintin. True as gold is Jerry Quintin. He always means what he says, and says just what he means. Let me assure you, there is no truer man in the Empire State than this same Quintin."

A few days later Sparrow found himself set ashore at Centerville Landing at an early hour in the morning. The first thing he saw was a plainly dressed man sitting in a buckboard who, as Sparrow approached, accosted him with the words: "Mr. Sparrow, good morning. Glad to see you. Expected to see an older man. Get in, we will go round and get some breakfast and afterward go out to the farm."

After breakfast they drove along the river road, behind an excellent team of bay horses, for a distance of about two miles, and drew up in front of a large brick house.

"This is our farm, Mr. Sparrow. We will drive on to the farm and come back to the house later."

Everything indicated thrift and prosperity. There was a great barn and stables, a capacious warehouse, out-buildings of all sorts, corn houses, hayricks, and a building for wheat, while nearby was a shed full of modern agricultural machinery. They walked through the stables; five fine horses occupied the stalls, while close at hand were not fewer than a dozen Jersey cows.

Mr. Quintin was busy describing everything - and he knew all about everything: buildings, their uses and cost; the horses, as he stroked the nose of each - breed, age, peculiarities. Each cow and heifer he knew by name and age. The machinery - he was familiar with its make and use as well as its cost. If his eyes had been bandaged, apparently he could have described everything on Monastery Farm.

They next drove back to the farmhouse. It was a substantial brick building, containing twelve spacious rooms, furnished with plain, rather old-fashioned furniture, and set back from the river road about three hundred yards; it was surrounded by a well-kept lawn, and in all respects, the place was inviting and homelike.

"Mr. Sparrow," said Quintin, "this farm contains two hundred and two acres of arable land, good land, no better, in fact, in the country. Besides, we have twenty acres of wooded land and a tenant house. This machinery is the best that we could find. We have two men - Giles and Ephraim; they are the best hands we know of, for Mr. Rixey trained them from their boyhood; there are no better. Mr. Rixey was our farmer twenty-six years. He died last November. Let us now have a look at the Monastery."

Half a mile away they came to it, a large five-story brick building in the midst of native oak trees; a wide driveway led up to the front door, while in front was a sparkling fountain. Another, a smaller building, occupied a site near by, and constituted the president's residence. The whole was inclosed with a tall iron fence.

Years before our story begins this land (three hundred acres) was donated by Richard Thorndyke, a wealthy Episcopalian, for a training school for clergymen, to which gift was added as an endowment fund one hundred thousand dollars on the condition that the church should erect suitable buildings. Thorndyke Theological Seminary was its original name; but, as the students as well as the teachers were all men, the people soon began to call it the Monastery, and in the course of years this became its common title; and the farm became known far and wide as Monastery Farm. This institution had from its inception found peculiar favor with the church as well as with the people, and the buildings were speedily erected. Two men at first were enough to do the teaching, as at the beginning there were only seventeen pupils, several of these students earning their tuition by working upon the farm. But at the time to which this story points one hundred and seventy-two students and nine professors composed the faculty besides the president, and the school was known as Monastery Classical and Theological College.

This inexperienced young Englishman as he saw all this became dismayed. This was too great an undertaking. He depreciated his own ability. This was altogether too big a job. He remembered that Nancy called it providential, but surely she was mistaken. What could he do with all that machinery? True, he had successfully managed his father's one-hundred-acre farm, but this farm was twice as large. There were likewise oxen on the place, and he had never handled a yoke of oxen. No; he would take the night boat home. Surely something more suitable would turn up.

He almost regretted having seen the advertisement. However, notwithstanding his lack of self-confidence, he presented to Mr. Quintin the letter which the preacher in New York had given him to be delivered to that gentleman.

"Ah!" exclaimed Mr. Quintin as he read, "this is from one of our best boys; you know him, eh?"

"Yes, sir."

"Ah, Charlie is as true as steel, Charlie is."

"He says better words of you, Mr. Quintin," remarked Billy.

"Indeed! What does he say?"

"He says you are true as gold."

"Well, I doubt whether that is better. That is Charlie's way of showing his appreciation. But steel is better than gold. I don't know of any useful thing made of gold; but what could we do without steel?"

They drove away from the Monastery and stopped in front of the farmhouse. Then Mr. Quintin, in quiet tones, asked: "Well, Mr. Sparrow, what do you think of Monastery Farm? Would you not like to live in that good old house? I am authorized to pay the right man seven hundred dollars a year, besides house rent, garden, milk, etc. What do you think of such a chance?"

"Mr. Quintin," replied the other, slowly, "I am afraid that it is too much of an undertaking. I fear that my experience is too limited. It would perhaps be better for me to look for a lighter job. I am a farmer, Mr. Quintin, and love the work. For four years I have managed my father's small farm, and have succeeded in making some money. But this work needs a man of more experience. Everything is on a larger scale, and I fear I am not experienced enough for so large an undertaking."

Mr. Quintin was an astute reader of men and had formed a favorable opinion of this modest young man. "How old are you?" he asked.

"I am twenty-six years old next month," was the reply.

"I'm afraid you are in danger of making a mistake. You may never have an opportunity like this again. The crops for the season are all in, and the two men on the place understand everything, and during this year you can familiarize yourself with the machinery, cattle, and all other necessary details. My advice to you is to take hold and feel that you are master of the situation as you soon will be."

Quintin, in fact, was so favorably impressed with this young man of twenty-six that Billy was finally persuaded to take charge of Monastery Farm, and in two weeks the new farmer and his young wife and child were comfortably located in the old farmhouse. And time had proven that Quintin had made no mistake in this selection. Each year had enhanced his opinion of the character and ability of Sparrow; the great farm had never been so productive, the cattle had never been more thrifty, and the revenue had never been as large.

Four years had passed, and well might Billy feel quite satisfied as he stood there in his shirt sleeves at the close of a certain day looking out over the farm. While he was thus engaged a young man, tall and slight in appearance and apparently not much more than twenty years of age, approached. He was lithe and seemingly agile; a thin, brown beard covered his face, which was cheery indeed, as was the smile which shone through two big brown eyes. His clothing was well worn, and upon his shoulders or back was something resembling a soldier's knapsack, while in his hand he carried a knotty stick. Halting at the gate, where Sparrow and Nancy and the boy stood, the stranger saluted them with a courteous bow. "Good evening," he said, "may I inquire how far it is to the next village?"

"Not more than two miles," was the answer.

"Is there a tavern in the village?" was next asked.

"O, yes, two of them," was Billy's response.

"I'm looking for work," said the stranger. "Do you think I shall be able to find something to do in the village?"

"What sort of work do you want?" queried Billy with a smile.

"Anything that is honest," was the prompt reply. "What I don't know I can learn. I want to settle down, at least for a while."

"Well, now," replied Billy, "you don't look as if you could do much on a farm. If you could, I might give you a job, at least for a week or two; only farmers or carpenters are needed through this part of the country. Could you plow corn or saw wood?"

"Well," was the response, "I don't think that I could plow corn, but I could saw wood, hoe in the garden, do chores, or feed stock."

As they talked the stranger unbuckled his knapsack, and set it down on the horse block.

"Where are you from?" asked Sparrow in a somewhat abrupt tone.

"I'm from - from - well, from every place, from New York last."

"Where are you headed for?"

"Well, sir, to be honest with you, I suppose you might call me a tramp. I'm hunting for a place to settle down in, as I seem to be without friends, so one place is as good as another for me."

It was now nearly dark, and the kindly heart of Nancy

prompted her to ask him if he were hungry, to which he replied that he had eaten nothing since morning. "I had a good breakfast," he added, "at a place called Tipton."

"Why," ejaculated Billy, "Tipton is twenty-two miles away."

The good wife had slipped away, and presently returned, inviting him to enter and have something to eat. As they entered the cozy dining room, turning to Mrs. Sparrow, the young man said: "My name is Edwards - Carl Edwards; I am an Englishman, and have been in this country only six weeks. I am trying to find some employment."

Billy, learning from Nancy that the stranger was a countryman of his, after he had eaten his supper, engaged him in conversation concerning the old country, during the course of which he learned that they were from the same county - he, Billy, from Barnard Castle, and Edwards from the city of Durham, which places were not more than forty miles apart. Of course Billy would not turn his countryman out to seek a lodging. So he was invited to remain for the night, which invitation the young man gladly accepted.

Next morning the stranger was found at the woodpile, busily engaged in cutting wood for the cook stove. Billy found him thus working as he returned from feeding the stock. It was a sultry morning in June and the perspiration was streaming freely down the young man's face. It was evident that this was harder work than he had been used to.

"You had better go slow for a while, Edwards, until you get toughened to it," remarked Sparrow.

Just then was heard the sound of the bell calling them to breakfast. Strange as it may seem, no more words about work passed between the two men.

Immediately after breakfast the newcomer found a hoe and spent the day in hoeing potatoes and corn in the garden.

Cutting wood, bringing water to the house, feeding the poultry, assisting in feeding the horses, mules, and cows, until, before the end of a week, both Billy and Nancy wondered how they possibly got along before he came. An extensive bed of watercress had been discovered on the edge of a stream that ran through the farm and each morning the table was supplied, and a fine bouquet of wild roses and other woodland flowers was found in front of Nancy's plate, while their odor filled the breakfast room.

Another change had come in to this kind and simple-hearted family. Tom - little Tom, now seven years old and the sunbeam of the farm-house - had begged to have his cot put into the room occupied by the stranger. Up to this time Nancy had been compelled to wash and dress the lad; but now he arose when Edwards arose, washed and dressed himself, and went downstairs, remaining by the side of his new friend until called to breakfast, when he would bring in a dozen or more fresh eggs.

So the summer weeks passed by; no word had been spoken about wages. The young man was now known by the familiar name of Carl. He was recognized as the general utility man of the farm. Giles and Ephraim, the two helpers, hired by the year, went twice a month on Saturday evening to Centerville, where Mr. Quintin paid them their wages. But Carl had so far received nothing, and his clothes became very much worn and their renewal was becoming quite an apparent necessity. One Saturday afternoon Billy invited Carl to go with him to Centerville, and there he was fitted out with a good supply of everything he needed in the way of clothes. So great was the change on his return that at first the keen-eyed little Tom was not able to recognize him, but a moment later exclaimed: "Ah, Carl, I always knew you were a gentleman."

CHAPTER III

THE PROMOTION

Rexford Mills was the manager of all temporal supplies of the Monastery - all food supplies, repairs, fuel, servants, etc. Three times a week his orders for vegetables, flour, corn meal, fowls, butter, eggs, milk, cheese, etc., as well as fruits in season, came to the farm. Hitherto to supply these demands devolved upon Sparrow himself, thus occupying much of his time. But during the seven months of his sojourn here, Carl had gradually and almost unconsciously become interested in the great warehouse and its contents and the triweekly demands of the family at the Monastery. Often the little wagon stood already filled with the order before Billy arrived, and Carl was found in the office crediting the farm with the morning's order on the books. This was a great relief to the farmer, as it allowed him to spend the time with the men upon the farm. So satisfactorily was this work done that Carl had really become the manager of this part of the farm's obligations. Once a month, Mr. Mills and Carl met to compare and adjust accounts, thus greatly assisting Mr. Mills in bringing an accurate report to the board of trustees. Mr. Quintin highly appreciated this accuracy, and spoke of it at every opportunity. Everything in the warehouse as well as upon the farm was in perfect order. This pleasant state of things could not long exist without becoming known in the family of students and faculty, and all soon began to be interested in the young man, the result being that invitations began to arrive for him to attend their entertainments and other functions. He was especially invited to the exercise grounds and games.

A literary and musical entertainment was to be given. It was to be a sort of Thanksgiving festival; the best speakers and singers had been engaged and they had spent much time in rehearsal. The bishop was to preside. The hour had arrived, but alas, where was the organist? No word as to the cause of his absence had been received, and a substitute must be found. Who, then, could be organist? John Keyes was the only man among them that was acquainted with the numbers; he had rehearsed them. But yesterday he had rushed away to visit his mother, who was ill, expecting to be able to return in time, and Professor Cummings was greatly disturbed because unsuccessful in finding someone to take his place. The president and faculty were approaching. They should now be singing the welcoming "Gloria." Instead, the great organ was silent. But listen! Someone had touched the keys. The audience arose simultaneously and sounded forth the grand old chorus, "Glory to God in the Highest." Few in the audience suspected that John Keyes was not at the organ. No one dreamed that the fingers pressing those keys had not during the last year and a half touched a musical instrument. But the festival went on with artistic smoothness to the finish. None was more surprised than the bishop, who at the close turned to thank the young man; but Carl had slipped away and was not to be seen. During the entire entertainment Tom sat on a stool as if he were petrified. This was the astonishment of his young life.

Next morning the stalwart voices of the students were heard as usual in their early devotions, but there were no notes of the organ accompanying them. Word had been received that Keyes himself was ill, and, strange as it may seem, of all the one hundred and seventy-four students none felt sufficiently proficient to assume his place at the organ.

"Who played the organ last night?" asked the bishop. "Why can he not play?"

"O, he is not a student. He is a young Englishman from the

farm, a relative of Sparrow's," replied the professor.

"Well, why don't you secure his services until Keyes returns? I wanted to thank him last night but could not find him. That young man is a musician, whoever he is. I will go over with you and we will see Sparrow."

But they did not find the farmer; instead, they fell in with Carl in the office of the warehouse. Tom stood on a box taking a lesson in penmanship. The copy was, "Honesty is the best policy." The writing lesson was being accompanied by a lesson in honesty. The visitors listened on the other side of the thin partition to what Carl was saying to Tom.

"Honesty is telling the truth," were his words. "Honesty means not keeping back anything. Honesty means telling a thing as it is. Telling the truth - not more, not less."

The grave bishop tapped at the door which was immediately opened by Carl.

"Is Mr. Sparrow here?" asked the professor.

"No, sir," was the reply. "He has gone to Centerville, but will return by noon."

"Well," said the bishop, "we really came to see you. You play the organ, and we are minus an organist at our chapel services. Mr. Keyes, our organist, we have just learned, has been taken suddenly ill and is in the hospital. Can you serve us until he returns?"

"I hardly know how to answer you, Bishop," replied Carl, hesitatingly. "I am working for Mr. Sparrow; and, besides, I have had no practice, with the exception of last evening, for a long time, which is, of course, a serious disadvantage. But if Mr. Sparrow does not object, I will do the best I can for you."

The end of the matter was that that evening Carl conducted all the musical services in the chapel.

The news soon spread abroad that remarkable music could be heard in the Monastery, and the people flocked there from outside to hear it, and the spacious chapel became crowded at even the everyday services. This new organist improvised such harmonies as they had never heard before. And this inspiration seemed to touch the faculty as each member of it took his turn in conducting the services. Bishop Albertson preached as never before. He seemed to almost ignore his notes as he talked to the people, and the people in turn manifested a devoutness never witnessed before by a Monastery congregation. Dr. Ezra Day had ever been a favorite, but the present hour brought him a far greater degree of popularity. The veteran Dr. Peregrine Worth also preached as never before. Indeed, everything seemed to receive new life; the old monotony had departed; something new had come. What was it? Was this what the Methodists called a revival?

So marked and intense was this feeling that a meeting of the faculty and trustees was called. Was this a modern Pentecost? So Worth said; so Cummings thought. A great meeting was held for consultation and the people were publicly invited. Everyone declared a church should be organized. The bishop was in favor of this, and at the proper time one hundred and eighteen persons presented themselves as candidates for confirmation. Up to this time what was known as Monastery was simply a scientific and theological seminary. Its faculty was composed of educated clergymen. It was a college with a bishop as president, supported by the church at large and the products of the farm, having a board of trustees to hold and manage the estate according to the laws of the commonwealth. Now it was to become an organized parish church and, in addition, the center of a diocese. The bishop was to assume the duties of the rector, with the members of the faculty as his assistants, and the trustees were incorporated as the "Board of Trustees of Monastery Church and College," according to law. This was a new regime for Bishop Albertson, who, years before, had been rector of a small parish in Virginia. Even at that time he was a rigid churchman and a profound scholar, and because of these and other qualifications he had unexpectedly been elevated to the episcopal office. Soon after this well-merited promotion he had been earnestly requested to take this young seminary under his care and superintendence, and had cheerfully accepted this added responsibility. From that time he had made Monastery his home and the head-quarters of his diocese. It continued to be "a school of the prophets" during ten years, when it was granted a university charter and it became a school of classics as well as theology. No one ever felt disappointed at this appointment of Bishop Albertson to the presidency of the institution, which under his care had grown from a small seminary with seventeen students to its present proportions and standing in the state. Now there were seventy-two theological students and two hundred and forty-five in the classical and scientific courses. This had been done under the fostering care and superintendency of the present incumbent. This institution had been simply a high-grade school of classics and theology, principally the latter. Experimental religion had but a small place in its curriculum or life. "Thou shalt not" of the Old Testament was strictly taught and demanded of all. But "Thou shalt" of the New Testament was rarely thought of, much less practiced. So apparent was this that critical observers used to say of it: "Here is where they have neither religion nor politics." And this local adage was literally true. The highest morality was practiced and demanded, but the dogmas which insisted upon the regeneration of the heart and life were very sparingly taught. Morality in its highest life was demanded of all, but the inner life was left to take care of itself.

But now, something had happened; here was a change. Even the organ spoke with a new voice; the prayer book meant more than it had in the past - everything spoke with a new tongue. Here was an amount of emotion that was new and strange, and the responses in the services were more prompt and fervent. The bishop ceased to read his sermons and talked as one who had authority. His voice was more distinct. The audiences heard him as never before. Several of the professors who had always been spoken of as unattractive and uninteresting became exactly the reverse. Young men were found praying in their rooms. In one of them the bishop was heard leading a score of young men in prayer. Old-fashioned and old-time hymns were sung, fervent responses were heard, and scores of persons from roundabout professed to have found Christ. During six weeks this wonderful influence was felt. It extended for miles throughout the country. During that time four hundred persons took upon themselves the obligations of the Christian profession and Monastery Church became a great power through the county.

Mr. Keyes, the organist, had died in the hospital, and Carl had been appointed in his place as organist and musical director. He very soon organized a choir of forty persons. And this was not all that added responsibility to this young man's life. The bishop, realizing the growing responsibilities of his work, appointed him his private secretary, which necessarily took him away from all the work on the farm; but even this did not separate him from the farmhouse. He continued to sleep there in "Carl and Tom's room," and, excepting during school hours, wherever you found Carl Tom was not far away.

The grand old man, Dr. George Thorndyke, who gave three hundred acres of land for a "school for prophets," little dreamed that his gift was to develop to such proportions, and become, also, a great influential church, a great center of religious influence, whose power would be felt miles around.

But the college chapel was neither fit nor large enough for the demands which were now pressing upon it. They must have a building capacious and suitable in which to worship. And now the true character of the great revival was seen in the prompt responses of the people; more generous were they than the ancient people who built the temple, and in the course of a few months a large and beautiful church was erected capable of seating twelve hundred people. As this building neared completion the building committee began to prepare for its dedication. The chief clergyman to be invited was an old friend and classmate of Bishop Albertson - Bishop McLaren, of Durham, England. There was to be, of course, select music; the singing must not be inferior to that which Bishop McLaren listened to in his cathedral home. Carl was told that the Durham singers were known throughout the kingdom as superb, and he must do his best in drilling his choir.

But there seemed to be, if not a lack of interest, at least a lack of energy. For many weeks before the time Carl assembled the choir for special rehearsal at least twice a week. And while progress was made, yet there seemed to be a lack of enthusiasm in both singers and organist. The cause of this was soon apparent. Carl was ill; and the day that the president went to New York to meet his friend, Carl was attacked with a raging fever. It was seen very quickly that the young man ought to have given up much sooner and the best medical aid was hastily summoned. Of course a substitute must be provided, and the committee succeeded in securing the services of Professor Schuets, from New York, to have charge of the organ and music during the dedicatory services. When the day (the Sabbath) for the great service came Carl lay in his bed delirious with typhoid fever. Nancy Sparrow was his faithful nurse, while Tom was hands and feet to his mother. It was really pathetic to see the little fellow as he sat near the bed so vigilant and anxious in his desire to be of service. And when the doctor came, how his great blue eyes watched his every movement! Then he would waylay the doctor as he left the house, asking if Carl were not improving, and if he would not be up in a few days. But the physician did not dare encourage the boy. It was soon observed that every morning and evening, immediately after the doctor's visits, Tom walked over to the office in the warehouse, where Giles more than once found him engaged in earnest prayer for Carl's recovery.

"I tell you, Mrs. Sparrow," said Giles on one of these occasions, "Carl will get well. Tom talked to God today, and I don't believe that God will refuse the little fellow what he wants."

It was on one of those visits that Billy, who was in the root cellar under the warehouse, heard the lad's footsteps and, slipping upstairs, listened to the prayer of his boy. These were his words: "Dear Father in heaven, maybe you are tired of hearing me ask you for the same thing so many times, but there is nothing else that I want; but I *do* want Carl. I would not have to ask my earthly father so often, if he could possibly do it; but he isn't able. *You are able* and, somehow, I can't understand why you don't. Father and mother and I all love Carl; he is one of us; and what would the bishop do without him? And now, dear Father, I'm going back to the house to see if he isn't better. I know you will do it. Amen."

The two prelates sat in the resident bishop's study. "There is a sample of my secretary's work," said Bishop Albertson, as he handed an account book to his friend, "and it is as accurate as it is beautiful."

Bishop McLaren started when his eyes fell upon the ledger. After a moment's hesitancy he remarked: "Never but in one instance have I seen as fine work. That was the writing of my own dear boy; those capitals are just like his. Ah, well."

On the afternoon of the Sabbath the two bishops strolled across the park, and almost unconsciously found themselves in front of the farmhouse. Little Tom sat on the front steps with a sad countenance; looking up he recognized Bishop Albertson standing before him.

"Well, Tom, how is Carl today?" asked the bishop.

"O, Bishop, he is very bad. He talks and talks, and they don't know what he means. He talks about his father and mother, and nobody knows where they live. He never told anybody. But I'm praying for him, Bishop, and I know he won't die."

"Can we go up and see him?" asked Bishop Albertson, and without waiting for an answer, he proceeded up the back stairs, but the English visitor remained below.

When Bishop Albertson entered the room he found Nancy bathing the sick youth's brow. She saluted the visitor with great respect. Carl lay quite still with his face toward the wall. Laying her hand upon his brow, Nancy said: "Carl, dear, here's the bishop come over to see you."

The sick man murmured: "No, no, he will never come to see me, but mother would if she knew."

The bishop in low, quiet tones said: "Carl, where is your father? We will let him know how ill you are, and I know he will come to you."

In still weaker accents the delirious youth went on: "No, no, don't tell him; he thinks I'm dead; better so."

At this moment Dr. King, making his second call for the day, stepped into the room, and at once in low but emphatic tones remarked: "Mrs. Sparrow, this will not do. Our patient must be kept quiet; otherwise more harm can be done in a half hour than can be overcome in a week. I will send a nurse tonight, and with skillful nursing we will, if possible, save the patient."

The bishop took the hint and quietly descended to the parlor, where he found his colleague awaiting him with his head resting upon both hands. Silently they wended their way to the bishop's study. It lacked about an hour to the time of evening service.

The visiting clergyman, addressing his host said: "Bishop Albertson, I think I have never told you the particulars of my great affliction. The illness of your secretary, and seeing the specimen of his penmanship, brings back to my recollection the darkest providence that has ever come into my life."

"No, Bishop," said his brother minister, kindly, "you have not. But sorrow passes few of us by in this world. We all suffer, some grievously. I did not suspect, however, that such had been your lot."

"Yes," was the reply, after a moment's silence, "mine has been a heavy cross. A little more than a year ago my son, just entering upon the summer vacation, went off with two friends on a yachting trip. They were near Land's End when a hurricane struck and wrecked the boat; they were all lost, the yacht never having been seen again; and once this afternoon, when the door of your secretary's room was opened for a moment, I heard his delirious cry, and his voice sounded strangely like that of my own lost boy. Possibly, I, too, should have gone up to see him, but after that I could not - I could not." He paused and then added: "O, it was my profoundest wish that Eddie might some day take my place, and be the comfort of my old age."

That evening's sermon will never be forgotten by the large congregation which came to hear the eminent English divine. "Thou destroyest the hopes of man" was the text.

Two days later the Bishop of Durham returned to his home, and although he had enjoyed seeing the classmate of his early years, the affliction in Bishop Albertson's home had reminded him of his own sad loss, so that when he arrived at Durham he felt prostrated by the renewal of his bitter bereavement.

CHAPTER IV

SLOW CONVALESCENCE

The new nurse would not permit even Tom to enter the sick man's room, so he waylaid the doctor at every visit, and, stern as he was, that professional gentleman was compelled through sheer sympathy to speak as encouragingly as possible to the lad.

Every morning Tom brought from the garden a handful of flowers and, tapping gently at the sick man's door, handed them to the nurse, who, giving him a more hopeful word concerning the patient, would send him with light heart downstairs to his mother to report the good news. One morning the boy brought a bunch of roses and violets, and gave them to Enoch, the nurse, who received them with greater cordiality than usual, remarking as he accepted the flowers: "Mr. Carl is much better. You shall see him tomorrow."

The joyous-hearted boy bounded downstairs and, throwing his arms around his mother's neck, repeated the words of the nurse. Enoch met Tom in the hall next day. The lad was dressed in his best clothes and was nervously impatient. "Now Tom," said Enoch, "promise me that you will not talk, and you must not cry, and, remember, you can only stay ten minutes."

"All right! I'll promise anything, only let me see my Carl."

But Enoch's patience was tried at the very start. Tom tiptoed into the room, and as he saw the pale smiling face of Carl and heard his welcome he threw his arms around the sick man's neck, and sobbed through his tears: "Carl, my Carl, you're nearly well, aren't you?"

Enoch, standing near the bed, placed his finger upon his lips, but Tom did not recognize his admonition, and kept on giving expression to his happiness. "Carl," said he, "God has given you back to us. I told mother that he would, and he has."

The pleasure of Bishop McLaren's visit was plainly lessened by the illness of the young secretary. The family of his host were all anxious, and the members of the faculty were visibly affected. Even the servants about the place felt concern for the young secretary and whispered many exaggerated stories concerning the case. But the crisis had been passed, and Carl began to improve. After a slow recovery he took up his accustomed duties, and church and school work fell back into its old routine. But six weeks of typhoid fever had greatly emaciated the young secretary. The buoyancy and brightness seemed to have left him. He had been fond of athletic sports, but now he apparently cared nothing for them. With Tom he would walk over to the exercise grounds and, seated in a chair, would watch the students in their games, seldom speaking and never elated.

The kindly bishop watched the young man closely and, after much serious thought, wrote to his personal friend, Dr. Marmion, of New York, inviting him to the Monastery to take a day or two of rest. Nancy exhausted her ingenuity to tempt and increase his appetite, but nothing served to help him, and what made matters worse, he seemed to have no desire to improve. True, he was just as exact and faithful in the discharge of his official duties, and in the correspondence, which was without dictation, there was quite as much courtesy, but it all lacked that freshness that had marked the past. The organ gave forth notes just as harmonious and perfect, but the music lacked the brilliancy and uplifting power that had hitherto characterized it. Indeed, his youthfulness seemed to have departed, and maturity, if not old age, taken its place. Previously Carl's full and joyous laugh had attracted scores toward him; now, however, a quiet smile was frequently the only indication that he was pleased, and even a sprinkling of gray hair was here and there seen among the curly brown locks. Once it had been a trick of his to leap from the ground to the back of Allick, Sparrow's tallest horse, but he now declined mounting a horse at all. The strong and springy step was gone and his feet shuffled like those of a very old man.

One day the bishop entered the office where Carl was at work, accompanied by a plain-looking man, possibly forty years of age. He was of medium stature, with broad and prominent brow, great brown eyes, and prominent nose. But the most significant and impressive feature of the man's face was his eyes - large, brown, and possessed of that peculiar quality which made them grow luminous when he was much interested and almost frightful when excited. He was introduced to Carl as Mr. Marmion, from New York. As Carl had no particular interest in the New York gentleman, after a few words of commonplaces he turned away and resumed his work; but the bishop having slipped out, the stranger seemed to call for the courtesy of the secretary.

"Take that easy chair, Mr. Marmion," said Carl. "Bishop Albertson will no doubt return presently."

"Bishop Albertson tells me that you are just recovering from a severe illness, Mr. Edwards," said Mr. Marmion, as he sat down in the comfortable chair.

"Yes, I have been quite ill with typhoid fever," was the reply.

"Are you sleeping and eating well?"

"No, not by any means. If I am gaining at all, it is a very slow gain. I have almost an aversion to food, and every exertion is a task."

"Ah, that ought not to be," said the gentleman. "You are surely not gaining if you can neither eat nor sleep. Perhaps your liver is not right. What is the doctor giving you?" Carl handed him the bottle containing the medicine, which he uncorked and after touching the liquid to his tongue remarked: "It seems to be the right stuff. I'm something of a doctor, myself, and I must help to shake up that liver. Who is your doctor?"

"Dr. King."

"Ah, yes - Hiram King. I know him."

The seemingly mere friendly interest of the doctor aroused in Carl no suspicion that he was the direct object of his visit, and that the conversation really constituted a diagnosis of his case.

After a short silence, Dr. Marmion incidentally, seemingly, asked: "You have no financial difficulties have you?"

"No, doctor," was the prompt reply. "Bishop Albertson allows me a very generous salary, and I have few demands."

"You have never been in the habit of dissipating, I am sure?"

"No, indeed; this is no place for dissipation, and before coming here, I was in school, where such a practice would have been impossible. I am as regular in my habits as when a boy in my father's house in England."

"Oh! Ah! You are an Englishman. From what part of England are you?"

"The north of England," was the short reply.

"Mr. Edwards, excuse me, but have you any great trouble upon your heart? *That* sometimes causes trouble, an actual physical disturbance, you know."

The young man, who up to this time had evinced no particular interest in the conversation, now hesitated, so much so, in fact, that the doctor repeated his question, adding: "There is but little prospect of helping the body, if there is a secret enemy affecting the heart and mind. This will always create trouble in the digestive organs."

To these words Carl replied somewhat nervously: "I suppose that, like most young men, I have regrets concerning my earlier life. There are some things that I am sorry for having done, and other duties that I have neglected, for which delinquencies I am sorry."

So entirely informal had been the discussion that Carl still did not suspect that he had been under examination. And the sagacious doctor having gained some information, quite as much, indeed, as he had expected in the first interview, abstained from pushing the matter for the present, and adroitly changed the subject; but while he continued to converse easily with the young man, he felt assured that he was on the right track. And when, later, he was telling the bishop about it, he declared that he felt sure it was a disturbed mind and uneasy conscience, more than any particular functional disorder, that was robbing the young man of his vitality. But after two days had passed, and he had taken advantage of every opportunity, he concluded that he would take the midnight boat for New York, his mission having been fruitless.

CHAPTER V

A CLUE

Two men sat in a secluded room on a quiet street in London. To look at the building from the street it would have been taken for a modest dwelling house. The room they occupied was spacious, furnished with several desks and tables and lounge and easy chairs. One of the men was large and white-haired, upon whose vest a golden star sparkled. But for this badge of authority he would have passed merely for a well-dressed business man. The other was a younger man, possibly not more than thirty years old. There was nothing remarkable in his appearance; he was tall and well proportioned with every indication of strength and vigor. He looked through large brown and sparkling eyes, a full brown beard covered his face and his head was covered with a heavy suit of hair somewhat darker than his beard.

"Lucas," said the older man to a stalwart colored attendant, "you can go now, and be sure to admit no one until I ring."

The speaker was the chief of the Bow Street detective service; the other was his youngest colleague. His name was Job Worth. He had belonged to the force three years, and in several instances had achieved more than ordinary success. He was known as Number 11. Job had graduated four years ago from Burrough Road Institute, and soon after received an appointment of secretary of the Legation at Washington, United States. In this honorable office he had spent one year, but the work did not suit his strenuous nature, and he returned home and soon afterward received an appointment in this detective service. Job was known in the force as quiet, self-contained, observant, patient, and was possessed of an extraordinarily retentive memory. Rarely was it necessary for him to say, "I have forgotten."

"Major," said Worth, as soon as they were alone, "I asked this private interview to talk to you about the bank robbery which occurred on the eleventh of last April."

"Well," replied the chief, "do you know anything new?"

"No, nothing certain, but I have a new suspicion."

"Suspicion," said the other, "suspicion doesn't amount to much. But what do you suspect?"

"Well, I suspect that certain parties got that money, and I want to submit the matter to you before I go any further."

"That is all right, Job. If there is enough in your suspicions, you shall not lack the authority to act. Proceed."

"Well," said Worth, "if the bank people will grant me permission, I can show them how that package of money was extracted."

"That," replied the chief, "might interest them somewhat; at the same time what they want is not to be given an exhibition of expertness in bank robbing, but to be shown how the money can be restored. In short, how it was taken is secondary to the matter of how to get it back. Anything else?"

"Of course, but I propose to show not only how it was taken but also to get on to the track of the fellows that took it."

"That is more like it," said the chief, quietly. "If you can do that, your reputation as a detective will climb pretty high. And there will be money in it for you besides. Go ahead."

"You remember," continued Job, "that just at that time, almost the same date - it was only two or three days later - three young men from Burrough Road (my old school) were drowned from a yacht in the channel off Land's End."

"Yes, I remember that incident," said the chief. "Judge Thurston's son, Bishop McLaren's boy, and another by the name of Blair."

"Well," said Job, "I don't believe they were drowned. I believe that the so-called yacht was nothing but an old tub that they bought for a trifle and burned, and then in disguise they left for foreign parts; in fact, I believe I know where one of them is."

"Just a moment, Job," said Andrews, interrupting, "has it occurred to you that every passenger's name is recorded on the ship's passenger list?"

"Exactly," admitted Job, "but who has ever examined any particular passenger list? And who, having robbed a bank, would give his true name? Then there are other ways of crossing the ocean besides a regular ocean steamer."

"Well," replied the chief, doubtfully, "ambition can construct many theories, but, really, you know, theories are worthless unless supported by something more than suspicion, and I fear your case is more of suspicion than of evidence."

"All I want," replied Job, earnestly, "is that you will allow me to follow my suspicions for the next three months."

"Very well," was the reply, "but let me advise you to go slowly. Be discreet. Remember there are other men also at work on this case."

"Thank you," replied Job with pleased emphasis, "I will

remember. Please prepare my credentials and arrange for my expenses; and," he added, "I desire a warrant for the arrest of James Thurston."

That evening, Job visited his club, where he was quite popular, and was received with customary good will. One man in particular seemed much pleased to see him. He was sitting alone at a small table, sipping coffee and at intervals emitting a cloud of smoke from a half-smoked cigar. Shaking hands with Worth, he said, as he offered his cigar case: "Mr. Worth, I'm glad to meet you again. I haven't seen you for more than a year. Won't you join me in a cup of this delightful beverage?"

"Thank you, Captain," responded Worth. "I shall be delighted. We haven't met, I believe, since we crossed the water together three years ago."

"That is so," replied the captain, as Worth sat down.

Captain Johnson was the captain and part owner of a large merchant ship, and had arrived the day before from New Orleans.

"How does it happen, Captain," asked Job, as he lighted his cigar, "that you come from New Orleans? Your trip used to be New York and London."

"Yes," replied the captain, "that was my trip up to about three years ago. I now make alternate trips to New York and New Orleans. There is more money in it for the company."

"I think you still carry a few passengers?"

"Yes; a little more than a year ago three young fellows prevailed upon me to carry them across. About that time I enlarged my cabin, and since then I have been carrying from four to twenty passengers each trip."

When the captain spoke of carrying to New York three

passengers a year before Worth became quietly interested. Accordingly, he inquired who the three young fellows were that were his first passengers.

"O, they were three young chaps going to America to seek their fortunes. Their names I've forgotten. The most I remember of that trip is that it was the stormiest passage I've ever made. It was a six weeks' voyage, and the worst of it was we could not have a fire, and, consequently, could not cook anything, and had to live on hard tack and raw pork, or beef. I tell you, those young fellows were unanimous in declaring that they had their fill of the seafaring life."

"Have you ever met them since?"

"No." was the reply. "We parted at the dock. I have sometimes wondered what success they had. They were quite young."

About three weeks later Job Worth landed in New York City, and, guided by an advertisement in the newspaper, he found a select boarding house on Clinton Place and engaged a convenient room with board for an indefinite term. Job represented himself as a gentleman traveling for pleasure - and information, he might have added, for his quest for the latter certainly took him nearly everywhere. Thus he visited the theatres, concert halls, casinos, and other places of amusement. He called at the private office of the Pinkerton Detective Agency several times, but nothing was accomplished. He mingled with the congregations of the more popular churches, with his mind and eyes upon the people more than upon the preacher, but without results.

One morning he sat in the reception room of his boarding place feeling somewhat discouraged. He was reading a morning paper, when a young girl, the daughter of the lady of the house, tripped along the hall holding several letters which the postman had just handed in.

"O, Mr. Worth," she exclaimed, "I want to show you the

picture of my last beau. He is a countryman of yours. He promised to send me his photograph, and here it is. He is good looking, isn't he?" And she handed the card to Worth. "I didn't expect him to keep his promise," she concluded.

As Worth glanced at the picture, he was startled, for his eyes fell upon a face he had seen in the junior class a year ago at Burrough Road commencement. Turning the card over, he read on the back: "From your ever true friend and well-wisher, J.G. Markham, Evansville, Indiana."

"What is your friend's name?" asked Worth.

"James Thorne," answered the girl. "Did you ever see him?"

In an indifferent tone Worth replied: "Don't know anybody of that name."

In thirty-six hours the young detective found himself domiciled in a quiet little hotel, the Mount Vernon, on the wharf of the Ohio River, at Evansville, Indiana. He selected this house because of its retired location. He knew that it was just as necessary for him to keep out of the sight of the man he sought as it was for the thief to keep outside the pale of his vision. He easily found the photograph gallery of Markham, but nothing of a satisfactory nature developed. True, the negative was at last found with a number 1,761 upon it, but no name, and the artist didn't so much as remember the face.

The hotel registers were next inspected without giving any clue. Now the young detective quietly took account of the evidence in his possession. What did he have to justify the arrest of James Thurston even in case he found him? And should he effect his arrest, the difficulty of extradition was still to be met and overcome. Could that be accomplished with the amount of evidence in hand?

He determined, in his uncertainty, to seek the advice of the British Consul, Mr. Harris, residing at Louisville, Kentucky, and accordingly he repaired to that city on the following day. The Consul recognized Worth's credentials and treated him with cordiality. When the detective had stated the case he said: "Mr. Worth, you can't arrest a man because he was not drowned, although rumor said that he was. What has such an incident to do with a bank robbery? It is hardly fair to connect a man's name with a crime merely because he happened to disappear about the time the crime was committed. Suppose a young man did leave England suddenly and secretly, and come to America? Maybe it was not *that* kind of a case at all. Could not even some unsuccessful love affair on the Continent have caused his abrupt departure, rather than the robbery of a bank? Mere suspicion is not sufficient to secure a man's extradition. No doubt your own good judgment will guard you against any hasty action, which could," he concluded, significantly, "prove a rather costly proceeding in the end."

Worth left the Consul's office somewhat cast down. He asked himself what next? Should he give it up? If he quietly returned, none but the Major would be any wiser.

Next day was Sunday and, back in Evansville, he wended his way to a popular church - Trinity - where the most fashionable people were said to attend. The structure was modern and capacious, seating about twelve hundred. The weather was fine and the audience filled the room. The music was good and the service pleasing, but the sermon was too long for Worth. He had slipped into a seat near the door, from which position he could secure a better general view of the people. Job at this time had a not overly vivid recollection of the man he sought, nor a precise idea of what his course would be should he find him. It was more than a year now since he had seen him, and then it was in a crowded hall in the midst of commencement exercises.

As the congregation dispersed Job also passed out, and took a position on the sidewalk, where, without attracting attention, he could observe the retiring crowd. The bulk of the congregation had left the church; a few ladies in pairs, still lingered, when the minister, accompanied by a young man of athletic build, came out through what seemed to be a vestry door, and would have gone by without especially attracting Worth's attention, but for the words of the clergyman as they stopped directly in front of the detective.

"Well, good-by, Thorne," he said, "I'll be around to chat a while with you in a couple of hours at the Commercial."

They parted, the preacher going in one direction in company with several ladies, and the man he called Thorne in the opposite.

Worth instantly recalled the photograph owned by the girl at his boarding place and followed the man whom he heard addressed as Thorne. There was nothing remarkable in his appearance, however, nor was there anything to remind him that he had before seen him. He was a good looking man, perhaps twenty-five years of age, of medium size, broad shoulders, and elastic step. He seemed to be in no haste, for he moved leisurely along his way. Every person he met seemed to recognize him, and he in most affable manner returned their greetings.

Soon a dignified old gentleman approached, and holding out both hands said: "Good morning, George. How is your father today?"

"Good morning, Judge," responded the young man. "I saw father just before I came to church; he is much better, thank you."

"Ah! that is good," said the old gentleman, as he passed on. "Give my love to him."

"Surely, I'm off scent this time," muttered Job to himself, as he slowly followed in the steps of the young man.

Entering the Commercial Hotel, he stepped up to the desk,

and turned over the pages of the register. Presently he found the name of George Thornly, room 104. Ah! this was the man he had followed. He had missed the last syllable of the name. It was Thornly instead of Thorne. He was now certainly at sea. Moving away, disgusted with himself, he walked through the spacious office, and almost ran into a man as he reached the door. Both men exclaimed in mutual surprise, "Hello!" Neither pronounced the name of the other, and yet both spoke it mentally.

Worth was the first to recover, and said: "Pardon me, I thought I recognized a friend; possibly I'm mistaken; my name is Worth. May I ask yours?"

"O," replied the other, "I have heard of you. You are connected with the Legation in Washington."

"Well," replied Worth, "I *was* secretary, but have resigned. Where have I met you - somewhere, I'm pretty certain. Was it in Washington? One is apt to forget names, when meeting so many."

With a slight hesitancy the other answered: "My name is Thorne. I'm a stranger here. Are you stopping here?" The young man was evidently nervous, and spoke in an uneasy manner.

Job, pointing to a chair, said, quietly: "Shall we sit down? We are both strangers." The invitation to be seated was rather reluctantly accepted, and there was a shade of suspicion seen by Worth on Thorne's face.

"Where have we met, Mr. Thorne?" asked Worth again, as if still debating that question. "Wherever it was, it must have been several years ago, if it wasn't in Washington, as I was there three years ago."

The young man seemed to recover himself on hearing this, thinking at once that Worth's residence in Washington had doubtless hindered him from hearing of any occurrences near Land's End or in London, and replied: "I'm an Englishman, like yourself. You may possibly have seen me, if you have been much in London. I spent several years in Burrough Road School."

"Indeed!" interrupted Worth, "why, that is my old school; but I must have left there before you entered, and I have only visited the institute once since I graduated. It is really a pleasure to meet in this country one of the boys of old Burrough Road. How long have you been in America?"

"I have been here about a year. I am looking around for an opportunity to invest some money with which I have been intrusted, but am making haste slowly in that respect," replied the other with a faint smile.

"Well," remarked Job, "your business is just the opposite of mine. I am looking around to *find* some money. Do you know of anything that I could get to do, in order to make some cash?"

"I'm afraid I don't know enough to advise you on that line," was the answer, adding: "Where are you stopping?"

"At the Mount Vernon Hotel, down on the wharf," was the reply. "It suits my pocket."

Just then the dining room doors were opened, and Thorne cordially invited Job to stay to dinner. The invitation was accepted, and they entered the dining room together.

This was a strange fellowship. Each knew the other, and knowing him was intent on outwitting him; consequently the conversation was abstract, abstruse, and uninteresting.

It was a strange phase of hospitality. When the meal was ended neither of the men could have told what he had eaten, or what he had said.

CHAPTER VI

OUT HERODING HEROD

While eating dinner the younger man assumed the lead in the matter of conversation, and it became general in its character.

"Mr. Worth," remarked Thorne, "you say that economy took you to the Mount Vernon. Now, I happen to have two beds in my room. What do you say to sharing one of them with me? It will cost you no more than you are paying, and I judge that the service here is much better than in your present hotel."

This proposition rather pleased Job, and the arrangement was accordingly perfected, and the evening found the two men genially smoking their cigars quite like two old friends.

This proposition of Thorne was not as generous as Worth might have supposed. There lurked in the former's mind an indistinct suspicion. Nay, it was more than a suspicion, and he reasoned that if this man was what he feared he was, he could parry the danger better by having him under his eye, for even now he was concocting a scheme of escape. On the other hand, Worth had no doubt in his mind that this was the man he was after; but how to proceed was the question that was troubling him. The words of the Consul still gave him no little concern. He had plainly intimated that extradition would not be possible as the case stood, and he knew that he could not secure them without the Consul's recommendation.

That Sunday night was an important point of time in the lives of both these young men. Some light wine was partaken of in addition to cigars, and each was thinking his own thoughts and forming his own plans even while the conversation was on other subjects. The bank robbery in London was spoken of, and in the course of the conversation the wreck of the yacht and the drowning of the three young men also were mentioned yet neither subject seemed of much interest, although Thorne remarked that he was well acquainted with them all.

Worth allowed the younger man to lead, and really direct the conversation, being all the while convinced that Thorne was trying to draw him out, trying to find out how much or how little he knew.

It was near midnight when Job undressed and laid down on his bed, with his mind made up that in the morning at breakfast he would arrest Thorne. The latter continued to sit at a table writing after the detective had retired.

Worth soon slept, and slept soundly. This was a new experience of late; but when he awoke, to his surprise, it was broad daylight, and yet the gas was still burning brightly. His head ached, and he raised up and looked in the direction of Thorne's bed. It was unoccupied. The instant thought that something was wrong, that something unusual had transpired aroused him, and he sprang out of bed. Just then a tap on the door startled him. "Hello!" he said, "come in."

A voice replied: "Can't come in - door is locked. Do you want breakfast?"

Job sprang to his vest, which hung on a chair, to find, by his watch, what time it was; but his watch was not there. As quickly as possible he dressed himself, and in doing so, he put his hand into a secret pocket where he carried his valuable papers, and pocketbook. It was empty. Every paper, even the warrant which the London authorities had issued, authorizing Worth to arrest James Thurston, and his pocket book, containing over a hundred pounds, had disappeared and he was locked in his room. In the midst of his humiliating astonishment, his eyes rested on a paper neatly folded and addressed to Job Worth, Esq., Bow Street Detective, London, England. Opening it, he read as follows:

> "You will doubtless be surprised on perusing this affectionate note. I know you, of course. I also know why you are here. When I met you today I at once knew it was all up with me unless I could outgeneral you - and I think I have. Part of the money you seek you will find in the bureau drawer. You are welcome to it. I have carried it around a year, and have not been able to buy so much as a cigar with it. Possibly you may be able to convince the bank that you are not one of the men who stole it. But, in return for making you so liberal a bequest, I have possessed myself of your watch and pocketbook. I trust that this will not distress you. My financial condition made it a necessity. I kindly fixed your wine last night in order to give you a good night's rest. When you arrest me be sure you have the needed papers. Good-by.

> "JAMES THURSTON, alias THORNE."

Worth at once drew out the drawer of the bureau and found at its further end a package securely wrapped in brown paper; but fearing there still might be deception, opened it, and sure enough, he counted fifty one-thousand-pound Bank of England notes. Securely tying them together, he placed them in the secret pocket which had been so recently rifled, and started to go downstairs, but found that the porter was right, he was locked in his room. After thumping at the door, without success, he remembered seeing a bell, which he rang lustily. After a few minutes a youth came to the door and turned the key. Worth, thus released, hastened down to discover that it was eleven o'clock in the forenoon. Within two hours a warrant for the arrest of James Thurston, alias James Thorne, was issued with a description of the watch and the amount of money stolen. A notice of reward was also issued and appeared at once in the newspapers. A general alarm was sent out by the Police Department, the railroad stations and steamboat landings were vigilantly watched, but without any results. Thorne had gotten away while Worth was asleep.

Fortunately, before leaving home Worth had sewed in the lining of his coat a sum of money as a reserve fund. This had not been discovered, but for which fact he would have found himself penniless in a strange land, with only his silver star as the insignia of his identity.

CHAPTER VII

"MICE AND MEN GANG AFT A-GLEY"

The return of Job Worth to London was not at all joyous. He sat upon the deck in his ship chair or lay in his bunk drawing darkest pictures of his defeat, as he called it. Nor was there any elation in his feelings when, upon his arrival at the bank, the cashier handed him a check for three thousand pounds, as a reward for the restoration of the fifty thousand pounds. Yes, it was something to be sure; yet not much. There was chagrin in it all, and he continually felt this, as he mingled with his colleagues. To him it was - well - failure. At this time, there was another meeting of the bank directors. Nearly all were present. The cashier presided. Something had happened again. Was it another robbery? But no, the atmosphere was different. Mr. Bone presented the case in a nutshell: A package had been received from New York containing fifty thousand pounds, and a letter had accompanied the money. It ran thus:

"MR. STEPHEN BONE, Cashier, Bank of England:

"Inclosed find a receipt from Express Company, which will be delivered to you, for the sum of fifty thousand pounds, which is one third of the amount borrowed from you a little over a year ago. Please to acknowledge its receipt to Express Company, and oblige,

"Yours penitently, ANDREW COURTENAY."

"This money," said the cashier, "was received yesterday and is now in the vault. Permit me to congratulate the Board upon having now received two thirds of the stolen money."

"Does anyone know who Andrew Courtenay is?" asked one of the directors.

"No," replied Mr. Bone, as the others sat silent, "I presume not. It is not vital, however, since the name is most likely fictitious."

Job Worth was given a vote of thanks for his services in restoring the fifty thousand pounds, and it was resolved that in each case where the money was refunded further prosecution would cease.

One day, soon after Job's return, he sat in his bachelor quarters, brooding over his ill luck, as he called it. So intense was his disappointment that he began to doubt his fitness for the calling he had entered, and to think seriously of resigning. True, he had been credited with two or three successful investigations, but this last undertaking could hardly be called a success. He had spent four hundred dollars in recovering one third of the stolen money, and had suffered the thief to outgeneral him. He concluded that he was stupid. Why had he not arrested him while he had a chance? But he had allowed Thurston to put him to sleep, and then possess himself of his watch and a hundred pounds of his money, slipping away while he slept, leaving him a prisoner in his own room. Surely Thurston, instead of himself, had played the detective. While in this despondent mood one of his brother officers made his appearance and was greeted with a decidedly doleful "Good morning, Nick."

But the other's response was more cheerful. "Job," he said, "I'm glad to see you again after your trip. I understand that the bank people honored you with a vote of thanks. That was a great thing you did in getting that pile of the bank's money."

Nick Hanson and Job Worth were of the same class in the department, and had been admitted on the same date. Nick was every inch an athlete, fearless and enduring. He was anything but good looking with his broad face, short limbs, and heavy body. He had made pugilism and wrestling his study, because they were his delight. Every man in the service respected his prowess. They all knew that Nick had never been out-classed in athletic sports. Yet, better than any or all of these qualifications, were his character and disposition. He was the soul of honor and gentle as a little child. He had a gentle and musical voice. Men used to say that Nick Hanson's laugh was worth fifty dollars a month. They called him "Old Nick," but no man among them was further away from that august personage in character and personality.

"Yes, Job," Nick continued as the two shook hands, "I came in to congratulate you on your successful trip and to welcome you home again. I think the bank has done the right thing by you."

It did not take many minutes for Nick to discover that his congratulations, while appreciated, were not entirely acceptable, and he went on to say: "Job, there was not a man among us that as much as suspected those kids of having done that slick job at the bank."

And, sure enough, this was true, and Worth unquestionably deserved credit for the original thought as well as for the ends accomplished. And although he had not succeeded in capturing the thief, he had restored one third of the stolen money. Surely, this merited the congratulations of all honest men.

Worth could not withstand the cheery words and more cheery laugh of his friend. Indeed no one could. None had ever heard Nick speak an angry word. He brought sunshine with him everywhere, even when engaged in the most serious work of his profession. He was the hardest man in the department to comprehend, and yet he was without a peer in frankness and good nature. Nick's genial spirit had somewhat restored job to his usual equanimity, and Nick knew it.

"It seems, Job," remarked Hanson, "that there were three of those rascals, and they divided the spoils equally. Let me see - Thurston, McLaren, and Blair. There is only one left. Is there no way to find out which it is? Two have been exempted from further prosecution, and I suppose the third one will be, if the money is given up."

"Would you know the third one if you could come across him, Nick?"

"Yes," replied Hanson, "I would know them all anywhere. And I think I could find McLaren, but since I believe he is one of the men forgiven - having given up the money - I don't want him. Blair is the fellow we want. Good-by, Job, I'm going away."

And it was four months before these two friends met again during which interval one of them, at least, had an eventful experience.

CHAPTER VIII

FURTHER DIAGNOSIS

Doctor Marmion, of New York, was greatly drawn toward his young patient at the Monastery, and as he saw him daily wasting away, he concluded that something more than medicine was needed to save his life. The secretary still dragged himself through each day's work, spending the evening in his room with Tom. The day after the doctor's arrival the second time, Tom being in school and Bishop Albertson away, he found himself in the office alone with Carl. He had hardly hoped for so early an opportunity to interview his interesting patient. But taking advantage of the opportunity, exclaimed:

"Well, Carl, you have improved, I hope, since I was here?"

"I fear there has not been much improvement in my physical condition; nor do I much expect any; and, really, to tell you the truth, Doctor, I am almost wishing for the end," was the young man's reply.

"Carl," said Dr. Marmion in earnest tones, "if you would give me your confidence, I feel sure that I could help you, and I will be candid with you. If you don't give that confidence to someone, it will only be the worse for you. Disease is not the only thing that kills."

"Doctor," was the quiet reply, "I sincerely thank you for the interest you take in me, but really your words give me pleasure

H. R. Naylor

instead of anxiety. Truly, it is not unpleasant to be warned that I have no assurance of life. I have nothing to live for. My life is wrecked, and I have not a friend in the world. Why should I desire to prolong my life?"

"Carl," said the doctor, "listen. Everything you say springs from mistaken and blind selfishness. Yours is the spirit of the suicide and coward; surely, this is unworthy of you. And, besides, what you say is not true. Your life is not wrecked, only as you determine to wreck it. You say you have nothing to live for. I know of no young man that has more to live for. You foolishly and ungratefully say you haven't a friend in the world. You certainly know the contrary is true. Everyone who knows you is your friend. Is Bishop Albertson not your friend? Is Tom not your friend? Is that sweet young girl in the other part of the house, whom you have caused to give her innocent heart to you, not your friend? By some mistake you have crippled your life. But the good Lord, who pities his erring child, will help you to redeem and make it both useful and happy. Bear with me, Carl, when I say, if you know that there is a way by which the usefulness and happiness of your life may be restored and redeemed, and you refuse to adopt it, you will be guilty of self-murder. Forgive me for these seemingly harsh words. God knows they are true, and my only plea for thus speaking them to you is my love for you. I cannot refrain."

Carl sat with drooping head and with tears coursing down his pale cheeks. For a moment or two he sat silently sobbing; his whole frame was shaking, and looking up with a woebegone countenance, said: "Doctor, let me come to your room tonight after chapel prayers."

"Very well; I shall be glad to see you," said Doctor Marmion, kindly, and rising, he went out, leaving Carl alone.

At the close of the evening service the doctor and Carl found themselves alone in the vestry. The younger man took from the pocket of his top coat a package, and, handing it to the doctor, said: "I want you to take this package and open it; it will tell its own tale."

Somewhat surprised, the doctor went to a stand close by and did as he was requested. The next moment he stood speechless with astonishment, for he held in his hands money, English bank notes, more than he had ever before seen. What did it all mean?

"There, Doctor," sobbed Carl, who had approached him, tremblingly, "is my crime; and growing out of it is my other and greater crime. I have been and still am a living lie. My father and mother think me dead. They have suffered - how much, I cannot tell. And my father was here. His expected coming made me ill; nor did he see me. Are you surprised that I do not desire to live? Father's belief in my death is easier for him to bear than it would be to know that I am alive and a criminal."

Then it was for the first time that the doctor grasped the full story - that this gifted, promising young man, lovable and genial, so attractive as to appeal to him as no other had ever done, should, of all men, prove a thief, one who had stolen a large amount of money from the great bank. The doctor was dumfounded! He knew not what to say.

Silence prevailed for a few moments; then the doctor's good judgment inspired him to say in emphatic tones: "Carl, our first step in righting this great wrong is to get the money back to where it belongs. I will see to it. You may rely on me, and the sooner it is done, the better. I will take the next boat and tomorrow forward the money by express to London. This will not be difficult," added the doctor. "But you have before you another duty equally as great. You must next enlighten your parents concerning your existence and whereabouts."

This was truly the most difficult as well as delicate, and Carl shrank back from it. "Is it not sufficient to return the money?" he pleaded.

"No, my dear boy, the return of the money is only a part of your obligation. No part of your debt must be left unpaid. To fail here would mean utter failure. Everything in this matter must be made clear, and then you will be enabled to begin life anew."

But Carl, with anguish in his tones as well as in his countenance, exclaimed: "*Must* my father and mother be told everything concerning my criminality? That he has a son who deserves a prison sentence? No! no! Better to let me die; better for both mother and father as well as myself."

"Carl," sternly replied the doctor, "you know not what you ask. Would you die with a lie on your soul? You said a moment ago that you are a living lie. Would you die thus? You are willing to pay your debt to the bank, but you are not willing to be just to those who love you with a love which none but a parent can experience. I am a parent and know all about it."

"Well, Doctor," said Carl, when he had grown more composed, "can we not do one thing at a time? Can we not take the money and send it to the owners, and suffer the other matter to rest at least for the present, until we conclude how to manage it?"

"Carl," replied the doctor, as he pushed the package toward the young man, "there is only one right way, and that is to become truly sorry for wrongdoing, and cheerfully and bravely make retribution to all parties you have injured. Anything short of this is not fair, and will do you no good. If I take any hand in this matter, it must be to right the whole. But, Carl, don't you see, you make no sacrifice in sending back the money - money you have been unable to use? Had you been able to use it, it might have been very different; it doubtless would have been. Its return is not necessarily an evidence of either penitence or reform. It is simply a confession of defeat. A coward can give up that which he cannot use to his convenience. And is it possible, after all you have said about being a living lie, is it possible that you are unwilling to pay any part of the price of your unfortunate actions? Penitence is like charity. It never counts cost. It is a godly sorrow for sin, and is willing to accept results, be they ever so bitter."

"Doctor," said Carl, in complete surrender, "Let it be so. I am willing to pay the price, even to death. I plead no more for my own sake, but I would, if possible, save those who love me from humiliation and agony, which to them would be more terrible than death."

"Here you mistake again," replied the doctor. "You imagine that your father's pride is stronger than his love."

"So I do," stammered Carl. "I believe that my father would much rather believe that his son is dead than to know that he is a criminal. There has never been a stain on my father or mother's name until - until I brought this one upon it and the holy office he occupies. Then, they have lived through the anguish of believing me to be dead, and it is terrible to think of bringing into their declining years a deeper sorrow. Ah, believe me, Doctor, it is not my happiness I desire, but to save them from deeper pain. If I am acting wrongly, I pray God, whom I now ask for pardon, may direct me aright."

"I greatly fear," replied the doctor, "that you are only willing to be directed in your own way. But I must leave you. The boat passes Centerville in an hour. I will take the money and send it by express on tomorrow's steamer."

As has been told, the money was duly received by the cashier of the Bank of England.

As Mr. Bone opened the package, he discovered that the notes had been first wrapped in a sheet of substantial letter paper, and sealed at both ends. As he was about to drop this wrapper into the waste basket his eye caught sight of a water mark; the letters were "C.A. Marmion, N.Y., U.S.A." Thinking that this might prove important, he preserved it for future reference. He laid it upon his desk and a few days later he wrote and mailed the following letter:

"London, May 25, 18 -.

"MR. C.A. MARMION, New York, U.S.A:

"Dear Sir: A few days since I received an express package containing fifty thousand pounds. The signature was to us unimportant, as we felt sure it was not the name of the writer, but your paper bears the imprint (water mark) of your name, and I concluded that you are interested in the matter, so I take the liberty of addressing you.

"Inclosed find an announcement we have made in many papers. The directors of the Bank of England have now received two thirds of the amount stolen April 11, 18 -, and hereby announce that the persons who have the remainder of the stolen money, if they return it, will not be prosecuted.

"STEPHEN BONE."

CHAPTER IX

HOME BANKING - A FAILURE

In the upper suburb of Montreal, Canada, stood an unassuming cottage, in the midst of a spacious and well-kept lawn and garden. A young man was seen carrying a rake on his shoulder and with the other hand drawing a lawn mower toward a shed in one corner of the lot, where he was to deposit them for the night.

"Hiram, I never saw the lawn look better." These words were spoken by a venerable-looking old gentleman with cheery voice, as he came around the corner of the garden, smoking a cigar. The speaker was a large and well proportioned man of perhaps fifty-five years of age. He looked through large brown eyes, kindly but resolute. His square jaw and firm mouth denoted will power, his face was ruddy, and his head was crowned with an abundance of curling hair as white as snow. This was Abram McLain, the retired member of the firm of McLain, Shaw & Co., the originators and organizers of the first steamboat line running between Liverpool and Montreal. From this investment and an interest in building the great Victoria bridge across the Saint Lawrence, Mr. McLain had accumulated a large fortune, which, promptly invested in real estate and safe stocks which were continually enhancing in value in this rapidly growing municipality, soon placed him among the accredited millionaires of Canada.

The cottage which he owned and in which he lived was built

of gray stone, one tall story in height, and crowned with a French roof. It was beautified by a wide door in front with colonial pillars and porch. The windows were tall, to which iron shutters were attached. The ground on which this building stood had been bought immediately after the conflagration of 1852, when Saint Mary's Ward was almost obliterated. From that date each year had increased the value of all property in this part of the city, so that this property alone, having five acres, would have placed its owner among the well-to-do citizens of the community. But this property was only a small portion of the holdings of Abram McLain. A unique building was this cottage.

Two skilled mechanics had been brought from Quebec, and no one was permitted to see their work nor to learn what they were doing. Their work was to be in the basement, which had been excavated ten feet deep, the massive walls reaching down until they rested upon solid rock. The building was seventy-five feet square. A furnace occupied the center of the basement. Next, in front, was a beautiful office, finished in hardwood, exquisitely polished, and furnished with most modern furniture. In the rear of this office was a smaller room, the walls of which were incased with steel plates, supposed to be both burglar-proof and fire-proof. This room contained a safe having no opening except the door into the office. It would never have been taken for anything but a closet convenient to the main office; but the door was solid iron, the lock of which none but the owner could manipulate. A reception or smoking room, which Mr. McLain called his den, was on the other side of the hallway - a cozy and yet elaborately furnished room, containing tables, sofas, and easy chairs, where the owner could meet his friends for business or pleasure.

Mr. McLain's father, a sturdy and sagacious Scotchman, had landed in Canada when Abram was about ten years of age, and began in earnest to win at least a living, if not a fortune, in this sparsely settled city, which at that time was hardly worthy the name of a city, although its thoroughgoing citizens had procured a city charter. Mr. McLain by earnest long-sightedness and industry succeeded in becoming a well-to-do citizen. Unfortunately, Mr. McLain invested most of his savings in a large banking institution, located on McGill Street - The Montreal National Bank - which a few months later was consumed in the conflagration. This unfortunate event with subsequent obligations, left him both poor and in debt, from which he never recovered, but in two years died, leaving his wife dependent upon their only son. Some years later, when Abram was accumulating money rapidly, he bought stock in gas and water works, and in both instances they collapsed, and the stockholders were left by a dishonest set of officers to meet delinquent obligations. This experience of both father and son not only met with indignant protestations, but drove Abram to a conclusion wise, or foolish, as the case may be; but he concluded that hereafter he would be his own banker, or at least the custodian of his own money. This accounted for the burglar-proof safe in the basement of the new cottage, and where he could keep every valuable paper, securities, deeds, mortgages, or money. This line of business was no secret in the community. He was his own banker, and when he sold property or anything else, the place of the money deposited was his own safe.

Much of Mr. McLain's spare time was spent at the Majestic, then the largest hotel in the city, he being its owner. Ernest Case, the acting landlord, took great pleasure in introducing him to customers, and especially if they were prominent persons or had titles attached to their names, who honored this hostelry with their presence.

One evening Mr. McLain sat in one of the cozy parlors enjoying a cigar with Mayor Dalrymple, he, himself, being an alderman. They had much in common to interest them, and were conversing interestedly, when Mr. Case, accompanied by an imposing-looking stranger, approached and asked permission to introduce Major Bancroft, of Quebec. The major took the liberty of correcting a slight mistake.

"True, from Quebec last," he said, pleasantly, "but from

Devonshire, England, first. That is my home, and you know an Englishman never denies his country. I am nephew to the Duke of Devon, and" - hesitatingly - "possibly the next heir to the title. At present I am a major in Her Majesty's Twenty-first Cavalry. I am just taking a run through your grand country, while not much needed at home. Gentlemen, you certainly have the making of a great city here in Montreal."

"We think so," said the mayor.

"Yes," added Mr. McLain, "we think that much of it is already made. We have already the best schools, the best churches, the best hotels and shipping wharves on the continent, and," he added, smiling, "the most beautiful women in Canada."

"I have no inclination to doubt your word in any one of those statements, Mr. McLain, and especially your last proposition, as it accords with my own observation; but my opportunities of looking about as yet have been limited, having arrived only yesterday." Then the major continued: "Is real estate increasing in value very rapidly?"

The mayor replied: "We have been burned out three times, but each fire has enhanced the value of all real estate."

"I am glad to hear that," the major replied, "as I am traveling with an eye open for investments. It is quite different with us. Capital invested in real estate in England usually results in regrets and loss."

This young stranger was a man of sturdy frame, broad shoulders, and medium height, having a military bearing; save his mustache, his face was clean shaven, and he had full lips and large, white teeth. He looked to be possibly twenty-five years of age, and would have been called good-looking anywhere. Both the resident citizens invited the major to call at their places of business before he left the city. This he promised to do.

A few days later, Case, in a joking sort of way, remarked to Mr. McLain: "I think some of your landowners ought to sell Major Bancroft something in the way of real estate. He has plenty of money. I have fifty thousand of his money in my safe, and he seems to be aching to invest it."

"I am quite willing to sell him some city stock, if he will give me my price," remarked McLain.

"But I imagine he wants something bigger," said Case.

"Why," muttered McLain, "I don't want anything better or bigger."

"Yes, I know," replied Case, "but I think he wants something that will grow while he is fighting the Boers, as he is looking every day to be ordered home."

"Well," replied McLain, "I give you authority to sell him the Majestic, if you can. I'll authorize you to act as my agent."

"Thank you," replied Case, "but I'm not anxious to change employers."

"But," answered McLain, "I'm not joking. I will sell anything I have, except my wife and cottage, if I can get my price."

"What's your selling price for the Majestic?" laughingly asked the other.

"O, well, let me see - I suppose forty thousand pounds would buy it."

"All right," said Case, as he turned away, "I guess I'll not change employers this year."

The Montreal Daily Gazette lay upon Mr. McLain's breakfast table a few days later. Mrs. McLain called his attention to it, stating that while awaiting his coming to breakfast she had noticed that the Albermarle was about to be sold to an English capitalist, who proposed to increase its capacity, and make it the largest hotel in the colony.

"Indeed!" said Mr. McLain, sipping his coffee, and he took up the paper to read for himself.

Glancing first at the money market, his eyes next sought for local items, and he read the following article: "Changes in real estate. Rumor says that the Albermarle is to change owners. An English nobleman who is looking for profitable investments is said to be the prospective purchaser. The capacity of this excellent hostelry, according to the report, is to be greatly increased by the purchase of the two adjoining properties."

About noon the same day Mr. McLain received a call from Major Bancroft.

"This is a delightful office," remarked the major, as he lighted a cigar that had been handed him.

"Yes, Major, I had an eye to comfort as well as to business when I built it," adding in a sort of casual way, "I see by this morning's paper that you think of becoming a property owner in our city; allow me to congratulate you."

"Well," replied the major, "your newspapers are a little too rapid. I notice that they sometimes get ahead of the hounds. I'm glad you mentioned the matter. Might I ask you how much the Albermarle is worth in your opinion?"

"O!" replied Mr. McLain, "it would not be right for me to appraise it, as I own the same kind of property."

"I see," replied the major. "Of course. What, then, would be a fair selling price for the Majestic? It seems superior in both locality and capacity."

"Well," observed Mr. McLain, "the Majestic has never been

put on the market, nor is it today for sale; consequently, I should ask its full value, if I mentioned any price at all. I would not look at anything less than forty thousand pounds for it."

"Would you not sell for thirty-five thousand pounds cash?"

Mr. McLain dropped his head slightly, and then suddenly replied: "No, sir, but I would sell for forty thousand pounds cash, English money."

"Very well, Mr. McLain, make out the necessary papers, and on one week from today I will pay you forty thousand pounds in Bank of England notes."

"All right, Major, I will meet you at the Montreal National Bank one week from today, at 12 o'clock. I will bring the papers."

"All right," said the Major, and departed.

CHAPTER X

ALMOST A TRAGEDY

A day or two after the sale of the Majestic, while the preparation of the transfer papers was going on, Mr. McLain's young man, who was acting as his secretary and clerk, asked his employer to be relieved of his present duties.

"Why, what is the matter, Hiram?" asked Mr. McLain. "Don't you like your job?"

"Yes, sir," was the prompt reply, "but I have got a place that suits me better, and, besides, I shall make more money."

"Where are you going?"

"Major Bancroft has given me the chief clerkship at the hotel."

"Ah, I didn't know that you had met the major. What will he do with Case?"

"I do not know."

"Well, it will be several days before he gets possession. When do you want to leave me?"

The reply was: "I should like to be released tonight, as Mr. Case is going to show me how to do the work."

"Very well," replied Mr. McLain, "come to me tomorrow morning and I will settle with you."

*   *   *   *   *

"Nick Hanson, Genesee House, Buffalo, N.Y., U.S.A: Come quick. Your man is here. Risis - Montreal."

Hanson received this telegram at seven o'clock in the morning, while eating his breakfast in the old Genesee House, Buffalo. In thirty minutes he was on the Niagara Express. That night about ten o'clock two men walked into the public room of the Majestic. Just outside the office door, in a lounging chair, sat the prospective landlord, as everybody called him. One of the newcomers was Ben Loring, a well-known detective of the Montreal department; the other our old friend Nick Hanson.

"Hello, Blair!" exclaimed Nick, in his usual jovial tones, as if greeting an old friend, as he confidently held out his hand.

At that instant, instead of receiving a handshake, he received a tremendous blow on the neck, just the place which pugilists aim for. Nick staggered and almost fell. This blow was not struck by the major, but by his new clerk, who had not been observed by either of the newcomers.

"Two can play at that game," muttered Ben Loring, as he felled Hiram to the floor with a sweeping blow, and in half a minute Ben had his nippers on the young man's wrists. "I'll teach you to interfere with an officer in the line of duty," he added.

In the meantime, as Nick staggered up, and the major saw him gaining his equilibrium, he succeeded in drawing a revolver, but as he raised it to about the level of Hanson's breast that athlete kicked the hand that held it, and the gun flew upward, struck the ceiling, was discharged, and fell harmlessly to the floor, while the dislocated hand of the major dropped helplessly to his side. The other wrist was instantly handcuffed, and within a few minutes both landlord and clerk were helpless prisoners on their way to the police station. Arriving at that place, they were duly searched by an officer and their pockets emptied. From the major was taken a receipt signed by Case for a package of money said to contain fifty thousand pounds. Then a doctor was found to examine his crippled hand. There was a compound fracture in addition to the dislocation.

It was now nearly midnight. After the injured hand had been properly treated and dressed the prisoners were locked up, and the officers returned to the hotel, where Case handed over to them the package of money. The two officers examined the notes and, finding them to be as the major had represented, departed with them in their possession, pending the proper disposition of the case. When they were gone the two detectives sat discussing the event that had just occurred.

"But who is the fellow that gave you the lick which so nearly put you to sleep?" asked Ben.

"O, that is Thurston, who is at the bottom of this whole Montreal scheme. He came here and learned that McLain had a safe of his own, and was the custodian of his own money, and knowing that no bank would receive one of these notes, since they have all the numbers, and that McLain would in all probability give no particular thought to the matter of the numbered notes, they both determined to risk buying and paying with this marked money, hold the property a while, sell out, if necessary for less than they gave, and, by selling, get hold of money that they *could* use."

"Nothing plainer," said Ben, when Nick had finished, "and tomorrow was the day set for closing the deal and turning the property over to the new owner."

"This Thurston," said Nick, "is the fellow that slipped away from Job Worth, taking Job's watch and one hundred pounds of his money."

Just as they were about to go to bed Mr. McLain arrived, and in the conversation which ensued made it clear that while deploring the unfortunate developments in the case, he really entertained no regret in having failed to dispose of the Majestic.

The next day a consultation was held at the Montreal Police Headquarters. There were present Nick Hanson, Ben Loring, the chief of police, the mayor of the city, two attorneys, Mr. Cross, cashier of the First National Bank, and Mr. McLain. The money was produced, together with the announcement issued by the Bank of England, and the cashier showed the list of numbers of the missing notes. The next point considered was the official assurance of the Bank of England that should the money be returned, prosecution would cease. All the money had been captured, or returned, and yet they had two of the men prisoners. What should they do with them? It was finally agreed to set them free. Before this was done, however, Hanson cabled his chief in London identifying Thurston as the man who had robbed Worth in Evansville, Indiana, but received the answer that Thurston would not be prosecuted. Upon receipt of this order both men were allowed to go free, and Nick in a few days sailed for Liverpool.

The major was taken to the hospital, but despite the most careful treatment two of his fingers were lost. He went from bad to worse, and was finally reduced to the state of a wretched pauper, but ever bearing the derisive title of "Major Bancroft." They all remembered him as the thief who bought the Majestic. Such was the end of a young man whose future had been full of promise, the brightest student of his class in Burrough Road Institute - a poor pauper, unpitied by all who learned the history of his life. Thurston secured a place to drive an omnibus to and from the railroad depot to the Majestic Hotel. He is now an old man, white headed, unknown, forgotten, unloved, and alone.

O, the pity of it! Two young men of good parentage and of more than ordinary ability, with gracious opportunities, wrecked in early manhood by mad and reckless ambition. Haste to become rich. And after the sacrifice of honor and self-respect and the securing that which they had coveted - could not use it for any commercial purpose. Thinking that its possession would make them rich they became poor indeed. They now drop out of our story, followed by our deepest pity and commiseration.

CHAPTER XI

AN HYPOTHETICAL CASE

There seemed to come to Carl some improvement in his physical condition; but there still came over him hours of great depression and despondency, when even Tom could do little to cheer him.

Dr. Marmion in his correspondence with Bishop Albertson had hitherto made no revelation of Carl's case. But the conviction came upon him that he, himself, was guilty of what he condemned in others and especially in Carl, in allowing the bishop to retain in his service a man who, in the eyes of the law, was a criminal, the perpetrator of a great crime. He concluded to write the bishop an hypothetical letter, describing this case, asking his judgment; and in this way find out what course the bishop would pursue if such a case should come into his life, and he wrote the following:

"MY DEAR BISHOP ALBERTSON: To whom but you can I go for advice in an important matter, which at this time is causing me much perplexity? I feel sure that your conscientious judgment will help me to arrive at an equitable conclusion. To you this may be hypothetical, but to me it is much worse.

"Suppose, then, a young man, well born, and so far well trained, at twenty years of age, away from home, falls into bad company, and, yielding to temptation, commits a great crime, but, escaping by a bit of sagacious stratagem, succeeds in causing his parents to believe that he is dead and mourn him as such, wholly unsuspicious in their minds that he has committed a crime. In the meantime he, in a distant land, lives a useful and honorable life, deeply repenting the sad mishap of his life, and fully redeeming his crime, so that no one but himself and the unhappy parents suffer by his unfortunate act. Furthermore, he occupies a most honorable and useful position, his employer, of course, knowing nothing of his previous misdeeds. Now, as already has been inferred, this young man is living a pure and honorable life, loved by all who know him; but he claims that to reveal to his parents the fact that he is alive would entail more and deeper sorrow upon them than to allow them to continue to believe him dead. He declares that they would suffer less in believing him dead than to know him to be a living criminal.

"Now, my dear Bishop, I write this note to you, calling it hypothetical; but to me, it is more than hypothetical - it is a real case. This young man is one of my patients, and I love him as dearly as if he were my own son for his noble qualities and his sincere penitence, as well as for the pure life he lives. His physical condition is indeed precarious, and I feel sure that his life will be shortened unless he receives relief. Kindly give me your righteous judgment of this case. I have his confidence, and cannot betray it; hence the secrecy of this inquiry.

"Sincerely yours,

"MARMION."

A few days later the doctor received the following:

"MY DEAR DOCTOR MARMION: Your hypothetical (?) note is here. I have read it several times, with increasing interest, and with a prayerful desire to be able to assist you to arrive at a righteous decision in what seems to be a very important matter.

"First. You say (if I understand correctly) that restitution has been made to the parties against whom the crime was perpetrated. That is well and so far satisfactory.

"But, second. The crime was a double one. When *that* wrong was righted to the first parties, then the second parties, in the deception practiced upon them, suffered more and longer than the parties of the first part, so that really the crime is only partially expiated until the wronged parents are undeceived, and he has made his peace with them. I feel safe in saying that this young man will never be happy, nor his physical condition improved, until he pays the full price of his sin. All who have been wronged must be righted. Depend upon it, his life will be chaotic, unreliable, and unhappy until he makes a clean breast of it to his parents. When he does this, if I were his father, I would take him to my heart, and give him a father's love and forgiveness. If I were his employer, and he came to me honestly confessing his sin, I should not dare to withhold either my confidence or my love. I should pity as a father pities, and I should say: "Go, sin no more."

"Now, my dear Doctor, in conclusion, this son (not you) should be the one to undeceive the parents. I can and do understand the *delicate reason* which actuates him in fearing to undeceive his parents in regard to his being alive, while they have and do believe him dead. If you can remove this deep impression from his mind, all will soon be right. *But he must do this himself,* not by letter either, he must go to his father; yes, he must arise and go to his father.

"Affectionately yours,

"ALBERTSON."

The bishop sat in his office six feet away from his secretary, while writing this letter of reply, and when he had concluded it he did as was his custom in his correspondence - passed both letters over to his secretary to read aloud.

In a few moments Carl picked up Marmion's letter. After reading a few sentences he halted, saying: "Bishop, this seems to be a confidential letter. Shall I continue?"

"O, yes," replied the bishop, "there are no names mentioned; read on. I want to know if my answer sounds right, and I can learn that best by hearing it read."

Carl had grasped the spirit and meaning, and he already knew what was coming. But he proceeded and somewhat hesitatingly read it through. Having done this, he was in the act of handing both letters back, when the good bishop, with a wave of his hand, said: "Now read my reply, please, *that* is the most important thing - read slowly, please."

The dismayed secretary felt that this was indeed crucifixion. Why had not the doctor spared him this? Did he not know that the letter would come under his eye? His first thought was to decline under the plea of nervousness; then, he thought this would be cowardly and unmanly. No, he would read, and at the close would decide. The bishop was a poor scribe, and his writing was always difficult to decipher; so taking this as an excuse, he plodded along slowly, and thereby gave himself a chance to hide his real feelings. But still he found this a difficult task, for his voice trembled perceptibly, and when he came to the latter part, where the father said he would welcome his son back to his home and heart, he stopped, his head dropped upon his hand on the table, and the paper fell from his grasp to the floor. The bishop arose quickly, and caught him in his arms, or he too would have fallen. In a few moments, with the assistance of Alice, Carl was laid upon two chairs. The bishop with the assistance of the registrar, who was hastily summoned from the next room, bore the unconscious secretary into another room and laid him upon the bed.

The terrible strain had been too much for the young man's weak condition. It was not long, however, before he slowly opened his eyes, and, looking up, he saw Alice gazing at him with anxious solicitude, while with her soft hand she was bathing his temples and brow.

Then all the circumstances came back to him, and he heard the gentle voice of the young girl bending over him. "Carl, dear," she was saying, "you are better now, and will soon be all right again."

"Alice," said the young man, faintly, "I shall never be all right again. It is too late."

"No, it is not too late, Carl," was the smiling reply, "you have many happy years before you. You are not strong. You must have a rest, and then your strength will return and so will your courage."

Mrs. Albertson came in at this point, bringing a cup of tea and a wafer, and succeeded in getting the patient to drink the tea. Then the bishop returned quietly and took a chair by the bedside, and soon both ladies retired.

This incident had been a revelation to the slowly acting powers of the bishop's mind; a quicker perception would have grasped the whole case much sooner, and might have obviated much trouble. But now the revelation had forced itself upon the unsuspecting mind of the prelate. Now he fully understood Dr. Marmion's letter, and, also, the cause of Carl's fainting. All his fatherly instincts were aroused, and taking the hand of the revived youth, he said, very tenderly: "My poor boy."

"O, Bishop," sobbed the young man, "Let me go! Turn me out! I have been a living lie to you and yours."

In his rapidly returning strength he arose as he thus spoke. "Forgive me," he continued, disconsolately, "and let me get away out of your sight. I will disgrace you no longer." He had secured his hat and moved toward the door, but the bishop gently detained him, saying: "Wait, Carl. Do nothing in haste. If you are sufficiently strong let us walk out into the park. The fresh air will help you."

It was a beautiful autumn day. All around them the scene was bright and peaceful. The trees were beginning to cast off their leaves. In the exercise grounds the laughter of the students in their games was heard, emphasizing the happiness of life and the joy of living. They sat down on one of the rustic seats. After a few moments of silence, and when Carl seemed to have become more calm, the bishop in a subdued tone said: "My dear boy, I am glad this hour has come. You have my sincere forgiveness, as well as my unbroken confidence. Let that suffice between you and me; I forgive you, as I hope to be forgiven, and I love you more than ever. But, Carl, there is yet another duty which you must perform. It has been left too long undone already. It should have had the first place, but it is not too late."

"I know, I know," interrupted the youth, desperately, "but it is impossible. How can I tell my father and mother that their son lives, and that he is a criminal and a liar? Can I inflict this upon them? They have by this time passed through the bitterest pang in believing me to be dead. Why now bring a deeper sorrow to their hearts?"

"Listen, my son; let me talk a moment without interruption. You are not *now* responsible for consequences. *You owe this debt and it must be paid.* It is just as much a part of the debt you owe - yes, just as much as the money that you returned. You cannot repudiate it and retain your self-respect. No man can respect himself any more than he can respect another who is able and yet refuses to pay a just debt. Now, you have paid your debt to the bank, and they have forgiven you. You have confessed your fault to me, and I gladly pardon you, and this confession and repentance enhances my love for you. Now, think you that your father and mother will do less? You are both unjust and unkind to him whom I have known and loved from my earliest manhood; and I must, also, add, that if you still refuse to pay this part of your debt, my confidence in your repentance will be lessened."

"Bishop," said the youth, slowly, as if weighing well his words, "I see it all now. But how can I do this? Can you not, will you not, write to my father?"

"No, Carl," was the reply, "you must, in response to your honest heart, do this yourself, nor must it be done through a letter."

Carl was thoughtful for a few moments. Then he arose. "Bishop," said he, "I will follow your advice. I will leave at once for England."

"This, my boy," said the bishop, also rising, "is what you must do. I was sure you would see it in this light. It is the only course."

At midnight Carl caught the New York boat, landing in that city in time for early breakfast.

Carl could not pass through the city without calling upon his kind friend Marmion. The Doctor was delighted to see him, and especially when he learned the young man's errand - that he was on his way to pay the last installment of his debt.

He prevailed upon Carl to stay with him until the following Saturday, and then accompanied him to the steamer Europa, on which Carl sailed for Liverpool.

CHAPTER XII

THE PRODIGAL'S RETURN

The Right Reverend Leonidas McLaren, Bishop of Durham, paced his room with nervous tread that was uncommon with him. He was *thinking*, and every few moments he turned to look at his wife, who had been engaged with a piece of embroidery upon her lap. The day was closing, and a soft melody from the piano, at which the young daughter sat, was the only sound which broke the stillness of the twilight hour. Frequently at this hour the little family found themselves indulging in thoughts of the sad experience which had come to them. More than a year and a half had passed since had been enacted the tragedy which brought to them their great trouble, and yet resignation had hardly been perfected - a sad lingering hope still clung to them even in the midst of their apparent despair.

"Tomorrow would have been his anniversary day," murmured the mother, sadly, "who knows, but that, after all, he may come back."

"My dear," said the bishop, pausing in front of her, and laying his hand gently upon her shoulder, "I think we mistake in trying to deceive ourselves. It is better to cultivate the spirit of resignation."

At this moment, Joseph, the house man, entered and quietly approaching the bishop, handed him a card. Glancing at the card, the bishop said: "Conduct him to the reception room. I will be there presently." Written with pencil on the card were the words: "A stranger desires to see you." That was all.

The bishop laid the card upon the stand by his wife's side and left the room.

The visitor's back was toward the bishop as he entered. He wore a long duster, and held his hat in his hand. The bishop's quiet salutation caused the man to turn partially around, and at the sight of his face the bishop started slightly and asked: "Whom have I the pleasure of addressing?"

"Father! Don't you know me?" burst from the visitor's lips, and then his eyes fell, as if he were overwhelmed with a sense of shame and remorse.

The bishop raised his hand in a gesture of blank amazement. Surely this mature man could not possibly be his son!

But at this moment his wife pushed past him exclaiming: "It is Edward, it is Edward!" She threw her arms around Carl's neck, and the next moment he was supporting her unconscious form, for she had fainted. The bishop recovering from his astonishment assisted Carl in placing her upon a sofa, and an instant later Eleen, the daughter, was at her side. The bishop embraced the trembling, tearful prodigal, but could only inarticulately murmur: "My boy - my boy - you have come back - you have come back! Can it really be you - Edward?"

"Yes, father," sobbed the young man, "I am, indeed, Edward, your son; but I am no more worthy to be thus called. I have sinned, father, against you and in heaven's sight."

"Sinned," said his father, still embracing him. "What of that? Are you not my son, and are you not living? O, how is this? We had so nearly given you up."

Nor was his sister's welcome less affectionate. "You are my

brother Eddie," she exclaimed, kissing him fondly, "and you are alive! You were not drowned. O, we hardly dared to hope for this!"

The mother's eyes at last opened, and she motioned for her son to come and sit by her side on the sofa. Then, with mother's arms around him, and father and sister near, he told the sad story of his fall, with all the consequences that had followed - the return of the money, and his confession to Bishop Albertson. "The Lord has forgiven me," he said, "the bank has lost nothing and forgiven my crime. Bishop Albertson has blotted it all out and loves me more dearly than ever, and gives me, as before, his full confidence. But all this was not sufficient to give me peace, and I have crossed the sea to confess to you my sin against you, and ask your pardon." The mother's arms were around his neck, the father's hands were upon his head, and Eleen held his hands in her own. All wept in silence a moment or two, but the tears were tears of joy.

Then the father spoke with trembling voice: "My son was dead and is alive again," he said. "He was lost and is found. Pardoned? Yes, joyously pardoned! Forgiven by heaven, forgiven on earth. My heart gratefully pardons all your errors toward me and mine. And now, my son, consecrate yourself this day to God's service, and may your future life be so loyal and noble that he who has been so loving and forbearing to us all and restored you to his favor, may at last crown you with 'Well done, good and faithful servant.'"

It was past midnight before they became aware of it. Joseph came in to escort Mr. Edward, as he familiarly called him, to his room, but the young man excused himself, since he had engaged a room at the hotel and his baggage was there; but tomorrow he would come to them.

He returned to his lodging, where he slept as he had not slept during one and a half years.

The next day was a great occasion at the episcopal residence. The early morning service conveyed the strange, but glad, news to all who were present that the good bishop's long absent son had returned, and they in turn transmitted it to their friends. He was supposed to have been drowned more than a year ago, and this day was the twentieth anniversary of his birth. The house was filled with callers from early morning until late at night. And thus it was for many days.

If anyone associated the reported drowning with the event of the bank robbery, they never so expressed themselves, nor was his whereabouts during his absence discussed in other than a friendly way. Nevertheless, the returned wanderer was not wholly at ease. He suspected that the kindly and refined nature of these friends silenced many questions which doubtless were in their minds, and often a lull in the conversation filled him with fear and dread of an inadvertent inquiry.

CHAPTER XIII

THE NEW LIFE

The chief regret now in this young man's mind was the loss of two college years. Bishop Albertson greatly desired his return to the Monastery to take up and finish his collegiate course, and receive his diploma from that institution. But the father seriously objected, because this would necessitate his absence again from home. After much discussion and correspondence, the two bishops concluded to leave its decision to the young man himself. As soon as Eleen learned this her woman's sagacity told her what the decision would be. She had her brother's confidence, young as she was, and he had shown her Alice's photograph. She was correct in her conclusions. It was not many days before he made known his determination to return to the Monastery and finish his studies. This would only take two years.

Edward McLaren now felt how irksome this change of name would be among his friends at the Monastery, for there he was known only as "Carl." But this must be met honestly, so he returned at once to his true name in all his correspondence. Edward's expected return to the Monastery was hailed with delight by all. Two great loves welcomed him: first, Alice, of course, knowing how much she had done in his decision to return to America, and that but for his love for her he probably would not have returned, gave to him her implicit confidence and all the wealth of affection contained in her womanly heart. Then Tom, who had been bereaved sorely for four months, was in rapture; he, however, could not tolerate any name but the old one, "Carl." Nor was Bishop Albertson far behind these two in his expressions of affection and confidence. All matters of business, of a secular character, were placed in Edward's hands and his judgment was seldom overruled. But, finally, on account of his studies, Edward had to give these up. So with great reluctance he resigned his office as secretary. This was greatly regretted by the bishop, but he could not conscientiously oppose it. But at the suggestion of the retiring secretary Alice was appointed to fill the vacant place, with the promise that Edward, when possible, would render her his assistance. And thus the collegiate year commenced. The number of students matriculated was larger than ever before.

Edward again assumed charge of the organ and was recognized as music director of Monastery University and church. Tom, too, was entered in the last year of the preparatory department. Edward and he still occupied the room at the farm known as Carl and Tom's room. This was a great help to the boy, as they had set apart three hours each evening for their respective studies, and the elder student rendered Tom much assistance.

At the close of the year Tom passed out of the preparatory department and was admitted into the classical course, and Edward McLaren entered upon his senior year. Edward was likewise recommended as a licentiate for the ministry. But the committee ordered that before this should be fully granted the old custom should be observed and he should preach a "trial sermon," and the date was set for that occasion. If possible, this occasion was of more importance to Tom than to Edward. He was continually referring to it and hoping that it might be a great success. The committee had appointed Sunday afternoon as the time, and the service was announced throughout a wide territory.

The day for the sermon was clear and beautiful. The bishop and faculty were surprised at the amount of interest shown. Many persons remained after the morning service, having brought their luncheons with them, and, as the appointed hour, three o'clock, approached, it was seen that the college chapel would not contain the great crowd, and it was concluded that the service must be held in the auditorium of the church. The large audience room was filled to its utmost capacity. It was truly an ordeal for the young man to pass through. Tom was the most nervous person in the twelve hundred present. "Will my Carl stand the test?" asked Tom of himself. But of course he would. Two young clergymen had charge of the opening exercises. Alice presided at the organ, and a full choir rendered the music, doing justice to the hour and the service.

The young preacher was pale and somewhat nervous when he arose to announce his text. At first he could scarce be heard ten yards away; but he quickly corrected the fault and went on with fuller confidence and courage.

He spoke from Psalm 119. 59: "I thought on my ways, and turned my feet unto thy testimonies."

"Thinking is royal," he said. "Thought is king. Everything of beauty or usefulness is the child of thought. Here is the distinction between man and the brute. Here is the cause of difference between the savant and the savage. And here is the difference between men. Some think; others do not. And what fields for thought are spread out before the human mind! For instance, nations and cities once great and influential are now blotted out. Babylon, Rome, Palmyra, Jerusalem. What destroyed them? They refused to acknowledge God, and he left them to perish. Ah! They forsook God and he left them.

"Again. Notice the nations that have come up out of barbaric obscurity to become the world power today - England, Germany, the United States. What has thus lifted them to their peerless position? They acknowledge God to be their God and King of all kings and all nations. Surely, then, this is a nation's palladium, just as it is the individual standard of character. Emmanuel - God with us.

"And to think of ourselves is truly ennobling. I do not mean as the egotist thinks. But to think of our individual capacity and obligations. The Greeks had a motto over their temple at Delphi, it was 'Know Thyself.' To know ourselves is the beginning of wisdom. Young men, learn to know yourselves and your responsibility; but none of these is the subject of David's thought.

"'*I thought on my ways.*' Our ways toward God. We have not treated anyone as we have treated God. We have shut him out of our homes, lives, hearts, while he stood at the door knocking; while he cried, 'Behold I stand at the door and knock.' Men live through years without thinking of God, until illness or affliction comes, then they call upon him for help. Ah! It is indeed humiliating to think of our ways toward our dearest Friend, who loves us and gave himself for us. It is wise and should, also, be profitable to think of our ways toward our fellow-men. We have not always treated them as directed by God's Word. How selfishness has inspired our conduct toward them in many instances! Who of us today can look back and see ourselves ever doing to others as we would have them do unto us? Who of us can say, 'I have always loved my neighbor as myself'?

"Well might this be the cry of David's repentant heart. He thought of a brave and honest soldier, whose wife he coveted, and in order to possess her he ordered the soldier to be placed in the most dangerous place in the battle, where he was slain. First, murder; next, adultery. Well might David's soul cry out, 'I thought on my ways.' It is not likely that I am at this time speaking to anyone who would be guilty of such gross sins as here cited, but you, citizens of this fair commonwealth, nevertheless, can well afford to consider your ways toward your fellow-men, remembering that no man has come to the full stature of Christian manhood who does not love his neighbor as himself.

"Now, in conclusion. Your thinking brings results: David turned his feet unto the testimonies of the Lord. Thought, if worthy of the name, prompts a man to do something or to leave off doing something." With strength and effectiveness the young preacher dwelt upon the latter part of the text, and closed with a warning against procrastination, declaring it senseless, dangerous, and, in many cases, cruel.

The doxology was sung and the people began to disperse, though many of those present pressed toward the chancel to congratulate the young preacher. The bishop, too, was generous in his words of praise, "The Lord thinks kindly of you, my son," he said, warmly, "or you could not have preached that good sermon. God bless you."

That evening and for several days afterward Tom was exultant. In his estimation no man had ever preached such a sermon in the Monastery church at the opening service, not even Bishop McLaren himself.

"Mother," cried the lad, as he returned to the farmhouse, "don't you think that my Carl preached better than his father?"

"I don't know about that, my boy," was her reply, "but I know that he preached a noble and practical sermon today. Yes," she added, "I think it was remarkable as a first attempt."

CHAPTER XIV

AN UNDREAMED OF PROMOTION

Three years have passed since Edward McLaren preached his trial sermon. One year later he graduated, and then came a surprise.

At the annual meeting of the board of trustees, the Rev. Peregrine Worth, D.D., Professor of Greek and Greek Literature, submitted his resignation. He had occupied his present chair eighteen years, but the infirmities of age were reminding him of the need of rest, and he felt that a younger man might be able to do better work. This was an unexpected action to the board, and it was thought at first that the retirement of Dr. Worth should be postponed, pending their effort to secure a suitable successor to fill the vacant place. But Dr. Worth remarked that he could not see any need for delay, as he was fully prepared to make a nomination in the matter of a successor. This, at first, startled them, and he was requested to state to whom he referred. But the venerable doctor preferred to do one thing at a time. "You must first declare the chair vacant," he said. "When you accept my resignation I shall, if you desire, nominate a suitable man to succeed me, one who will, I feel certain, receive the unanimous vote of this Board."

After some discussion it was moved and seconded that Dr. Worth's resignation be accepted with regret. The motion carried and the chair was declared vacant. Then it was that Mr.

H. R. Naylor

J.M. Quintin arose and moved that they at once proceed to elect a man to fill the vacant chair. After some debate, this motion prevailed. Dr. Worth then arose and said: "It now becomes my privilege, as well as pleasure, to put in nomination the name of a man whom I deem fully competent to fill the vacant chair. One who has just graduated with honor and esteem. He is a conscientious student, a thorough scholar, and an able preacher. It gives me pleasure to present the name of Edward McLaren for the chair of Greek in this Institution."

The fact that he had but just graduated had shut him out of their minds as a probable candidate. While there was nothing objectionable in the man named save his youth and inexperience, still the nomination was productive of no little surprise. The bishop, although secretly indorsing the nomination, feared for its success because of its being sprung upon them so suddenly, so he suggested its postponement until next day. But Mr. Quintin arose and expressed his belief that they were as well prepared to decide the matter then as they would be tomorrow. As for himself, he was glad he had the privilege of seconding the nomination of this young man, whom he had known for some time and most favorably. His remarks created a good impression, and after due deliberation the vote was taken and Edward McLaren was declared unanimously elected to occupy the chair of Greek and Greek Literature in Monastery University.

That evening the president's banquet was a season of universal rejoicing. The president, the retiring professor, Dr. Worth, and the new professor welcomed the many guests.

The courtship of Edward McLaren and Alice Albertson was not of the usual character. In this instance love did run smoothly. It was such a union of souls as needed no rapturous expressions. It was made up of esteem, appreciation, and confidence, resulting in simple, sincere affection that was unselfish and unflinching.

A formal betrothal had seemed scarcely necessary. From their first meeting their love had been mutual. Every glance of the eye, every word of the lip, was a pledge of loyalty and affection. There was no fearful ordeal of gaining her father's consent. They simply loved each other unfalteringly, strongly, devotedly, and the bishop and his wife were wise enough to see and heed.

And their marriage was of a similar unique character. No great announcements were sent out. Bishop Albertson simply invited his many friends to witness the ceremony, and the University Chapel, in which the ceremony was performed, was filled to its utmost capacity. No presents were accepted. Bishop McLaren and Eleen crossed the ocean for the occasion, and a warm welcome was given them by the great circle of friends. Tom was Edward's best man, and Eleen was Alice's brides-maid. The great choir sang the grand old "Marriage Jubilate," and the two bishops made them one.

Edward and Alice accompanied the Bishop and Eleen to Durham, making this their bridal trip, returning by way of London, being absent two months.

Upon their return there was no choice left them but to live with Alice's parents, at the Bishop's residence, which was a joy to the parental hearts as well as a great pleasure to the newly-married couple.

CHAPTER XV

TEN YEARS LATER

The Monastery Church has assumed the size and somewhat the character of a cathedral and the good bishop has begun to feel the irksomeness of his accumulating labors. True, he is able to attend to his episcopal duties, but even they have in many instances been laid upon his gifted son-in-law. This has been almost entirely true of the University superintendency, so much so, in fact, that McLaren has acquired the title of Dean and is now seldom, addressed by, or spoken of, by any other official title than Dean.

Alice has become quite matronly, and her two boys, Leonidas and Tom, make cheerful the episcopal residence, and enliven the episcopal heart. The students in the preparatory department speak of her as Mother McLaren, because of her sweet and loving guardianship; and the older students bring their trouble and confidences to her for comfort and advice. Tom Sparrow, after he graduated, spent three years at Heidelberg and won the degree of Ph.D. But while these honors came to Tom, and still greater honors had come to McLaren, they were still the same to each other. To Tom, McLaren, although addressed as "Doctor" by others, was still "my Carl," and in return the younger man to McLaren was simply "Tom." Nothing seemed able to change these relations; nor did the parties most deeply interested desire to change them.

Tom in his travels had been to Durham. Yes, it turned out that he had spent *much* of his spare time in that ancient city, and that his home at those visits was usually at the episcopal residence.

Tom and Eleen had met at McLaren's wedding, and it did not take long for the old, old story to find a place in their lives. Of course anyone from America who was acquainted with their son was welcomed by the bishop and his wife. But knowing the intimate relations existing between these two, Tom was made doubly welcome. Besides this, Tom had developed into a splendid man in both body and mind. He was six feet high and well proportioned. He had inherited a healthy constitution, lived a clean and natural life, and was in the best sense a handsome man, one whom in passing you would incline to glance at a second time. He soon became quite popular at Heidelberg with both lecturers and students, so when he visited Barnard's Castle, the family of Grandpa Sparrow, received Billy's son with open arms and hearts. The unsophisticated old people just sat and looked at him and listened to his words about his father and mother, and the great farm which he was operating so successfully. Cliff Farm was a little more than a mile from Barnard's Castle, and as Elder Sparrow was very popular with the people, many of them came to see Billy's son, both young men and maidens, and many a delightful time they had together. Though gifted with personal grace of person, Tom's real attractiveness was his naturalness. He was just as simple and natural as when, years ago, he went to the warehouse and talked to God about Carl. And so, now at twenty-one, he had a pleasant greeting and a happy word for everyone. The young girls were charmed and the young men listened admiringly. He talked to the young farmers about farming. Horses, breeds of cows, sheep hogs, fertilizers, until the young men went away feeling that they knew but little about real farming.

The aged rector of Ascension Church, who had known Billy when a child, came to Cliff Farm to see Billy's son. He likewise knew something of the Monastery, and more about Bishop Albertson, with whom he had been associated in his collegiate days at Oxford. The aged clergyman was much interested in the curriculum at Monastery University, and perhaps no one was better able to satisfy his quest than Tom. Tom might safely have written, if such had been his ambition, "Veni, vidi vici," but nothing of this spirit inspired this young man of nature; and perhaps while he would not have been adjudged a remarkable scholar, yet he was an encyclopedia of general information, and out of the fullness of a healthy heart and memory his mouth spoke to the edification and enjoyment of all who heard him.

We have said that Tom was not a remarkable scholar; yet he was a scholar, he was cyclopaedic. He had a general knowledge, and never forgot anything. He was an unconscious student all the time.

But his attractiveness was not in his scholarship, but in his heart and character. He possessed and was actuated by an unselfish and clean heart and a pure conscience. He did not need to write upon his hat, I am a Christian. The Golden Rule was the standard of his life and he was hardly conscious of it.

CHAPTER XVI

THE FAREWELL COMMENCEMENT

Commencement exercises this year were very interesting; more than ordinarily so. There were twenty-two graduates in the classical course, and twenty-seven seniors in the theological class. There were four hundred and sixty students in all. This was a much larger number than in any preceding year. Nothing had occurred during the year to mar the peace of the institution. Sixteen professors, clothed in their official garments, with the president, occupied the platform, which was profusely decorated with plants and cut flowers, while an immense American flag floated over the president's table. But, somehow, there was a feeling of sadness pervading the whole program; probably no one could have told what caused it.

The four addresses, delivered by as many graduates, were of a high order - vivacious, brilliant, and one or two of them quite exhilarating and fine. Yet there was prevalent something like the feeling of a funeral occasion - a feeling which follows the loss of a friend. But no one was dead. Even the applause at the end of any well-given number was gentle and subdued. The president and Professor McLaren presented the diplomas. After the graduating classes were again seated the president arose to deliver his annual address.

This was Bishop Albertson's thirtieth time during his presidential career. How changed since he delivered the first address to seventeen students, and with only three professors by his side! Now four hundred and sixty students in his audience; sixteen professors sat by his side and he had just delivered forty-nine diplomas to as many graduates. Usually the annual address was mainly to the graduates. This address took a wider scope. It was intended and did touch everyone who had an interest in this great institution. It was full of affectionate counsel and expressions of honest gratitude. The atmosphere which had been unconsciously affecting the people throughout the program was beginning to be analyzed. Farewell words were of course expected at this time; such were customary at such a time. But these were no common words. There was more than a common "Good-by" in them. This president had spoken similar words twenty-nine times, but never just such words. His eyes were growing misty when at the end he said: "My dear friends, this is not simply a 'Good-by' that I speak, but a sincere, heartfelt 'Farewell.'" A few minutes later seven hundred persons stood with eyes suffused with tears, and with bowed heads to receive the apostolic benediction.

Next day at ten o'clock the joint board met in the board room, in its annual meeting. The attendance was large - trustees, faculty, and visiting brethren. The word had gone out that important changes would likely take place, but none knew just what they would be.

J. M. Quintin, chairman of the board, presided. Reports from each officer were made. The secretary of the board read his report; it was a model of perspicuity and encouragement. Each member of the faculty presented an account of his work. A glowing report was made by Quintin of Sparrow's work on the farm, and a resolution of appreciation was sent to the farmer. Indeed, the board had never received such reports of the prosperous condition of the Monastery. Then came the president's annual report. This was his thirtieth annual report; nor was it very different from the twenty-nine that had preceded it. It was permeated with hopefulness for the future and gratitude for the past. Then came that which seemed to be the great burden of his heart. This was to be his last official message. He said, in substance, that the wise man's description of old age was fast coming into his experience. The keepers of the house begin to tremble, the grinders were ceasing because they were few. He was beginning to be afraid of that which was high. The almond was flourishing; the grasshopper was becoming a burden; desire was beginning to fail. In a word, three score and ten years reminded him that he must be relieved of some of his official burdens. He did not dare to interfere with his episcopal duties, feeling that possibly for a year or two more he might be able to meet and discharge them. But that from the arduous duties of the University he must be relieved and a younger man asked to become its president. And he wished that these remarks be considered as his positive resignation as president of Monastery University.

It was now four o'clock. They had been in session since ten o'clock. So, by motion, they, without remarks, adjourned to meet at seven o'clock in the evening.

In reality the president's resignation was a surprise to many. "What now?" was the question. As the hour approached the men were seen in groups, engaged in earnest discussion. But when they came together it was soon manifest that there was no concert of thought, much less readiness for concert of action. The prevailing thought seemed to be to postpone any attempt to elect a president, it being the feeling that it was too precipitous. But a majority of the board insisted on at once proceeding to fill the vacant presidency, their chief argument being that the new incumbent might have time to prepare for the fall term, and, further, that no outside parties might be formed and no politics should be allowed to interfere.

Bishop Albertson was asked to preside, and when the board was called to order, Mr. Quintin arose and modestly asked permission to address them. All were glad to hear this faithful servant of the institution.

He begged them not to construe his remarks into self-praise, but to understand them as intending to simply show his unselfish interest in the prosperity of the Monastery. Only this and nothing more. Thirty-one years ago he had been made a trustee. He was then nineteen years of age, and at their first meeting he was elected treasurer of said board. From, that date every dollar received or paid out in the interest of this institution had passed through his hands. He had planned every building and paid for its erection; laid off the Monastery Park, superintended the farm, stocked it with all its live stock, purchased and paid for all the agricultural implements. He had planned, built and paid for the erection of the new church building. He had charge of Mr. Thorndyke's endowment fund, to which had been added fifty thousand dollars, making now one hundred and fifty thousand dollars, which was safely invested at six per cent interest per annum. All this had been simply a labor of love, he never having received a dollar for his services. This was not boasting, but simply to show them his love for the interests of Monastery University and church. And this love alone inspired him to nominate a man for the vacant presidency. And to still further gain their confidence in his unselfish judgment and love, he continued: "Seventeen years ago, when Mr. Rixey died, I engaged a young man twenty-six years of age to work our farm. Surely I made no mistake. There is no better man than William Sparrow, and no better farm in the county. Ten years ago, I made bold to nominate a man for the place made vacant by the resignation of Dr. Worth. Did I make any mistake in that nomination? Did you make any mistake in confirming that nomination? And now our beloved president is retiring, full of honors and esteem, and that great and responsible place is vacant, and I confess that my past successes make me confident as I pronounce the name of a successor. I have consulted no man, not even the man whose name I shall speak. I do not know but he may decline the nomination, but my best judgment and unbiased conscience unite and prompt me to nominate Edward McLaren, LL.D., for presidency of Monastery University."

This nomination did not seem to surprise anyone except the man nominated. The thought of such an occurrence had not so much as come to him. Several weeks before the bishop had in an incidental way intimated that he was seriously contemplating shaking off some of his responsibilities, but nothing more had been said, and Edward had forgotten the remark. And when the bishop had presented his resignation, and it was accepted, McLaren simply concluded that this would entail extra work upon him for a month or two, until the trustees found a suitable man to fill the vacancy. But now as he heard his name spoken, it came like an electric shock, and he sprang to his feet, exclaiming: "O, no! This must not be. It cannot be!" He then moved a postponement of the election. He said: "It is only thirteen years since I stood in front of that old farmhouse, tired and hungry, a timid wandering youth, seeking work and bread, but more, seeking rest of soul and conscience. The farmer and his precious wife took me in and have been to me more than brother and sister." Then, turning round and facing the bishop, he continued: "And this man has been more than a father; but for him and the wife he gave me, I should not be here today. No! no! You have honored me too much already, and I move a postponement of this election until a future meeting of the board of trustees."

There was not a man but what was affected by these unselfish and grateful words; but they affected the auditors in just the opposite direction from that intended - really they insured his election.

A moment of silence followed. Then Mr. Quintin arose and said. "Mr. President, I hear no second to Dr. McLaren's motion to postpone. His words have indeed touched my heart, and in their modesty and unselfishness I see only a confirmation that I am making a wise nomination. I am thoroughly convinced that I am commending the right man, and with all due respect to the opinion of Dr. McLaren, I now renew my nomination."

The chairman, with his usual dignity, put the question, and Edward McLaren, LL.D., was unanimously elected president of Monastery University.

H. R. Naylor

Such election of course created another vacancy in the faculty of the Monastery. The chairman proceeded at once to state this fact. Again there was silence.

"Cannot the work of this chair be divided among the other professors for a time?" asked Professor Ware, the Professor of Belles-Lettres.

Mr. Smithson, one of the trustees, moved to adjourn, but the motion was defeated by a large majority.

"What now is the pleasure of the board?" asked the chairman. Then someone moved to proceed at once to the election of a professor to fill the vacant chair of Greek and Greek Literature.

This motion prevailed, and the chair announced its readiness to hear nominations for the vacant chair.

Abram Smithson, Jr., son of one of the trustees, who graduated the day before, was nominated. But this nomination met with no second.

There were some indications of surprise, which brought Professor Cummins to his feet, and with some asperity to say that he saw no reasons for expressions of surprise. It was certainly not the first time that this chair had been filled by a man who had recently graduated. This made several men smile, among them McLaren, who had been elected to fill that chair the day after his graduation.

Then the bishop stated that during the thirty years in the past he had never made a nomination, but that he now felt inclined to do so; and he would nominate Thomas Sparrow, Ph.D., for the vacant chair of Greek and Greek Literature. Sparrow was one of their own graduates. First, in their preparatory course; then in classics, and afterward three years in Heidelberg, where he had won the Philosophy Doctorate.

At this moment the newly-elected president who had been

sitting with drooping head, as if he had been rebuked instead of having received their highest honor, arose and stated that he would be greatly pleased if Dr. Sparrow could be elected to fill the vacant chair, but he feared they were too late. Forty-eight hours ago the joint board of Burrough Road Institute, a noted school in London, had elected him to fill the chair of Belles-Lettres and History, and he feared that Sparrow had before now telegraphed his acceptance.

"Then," said Quintin, "I move that we elect him anyhow - even if I have to cross the sea to give Burrough Road satisfaction."

The inspiration was complete; every man was ready to vote, and did vote for the man who was wanted in London - and Tom Sparrow became Dr. Sparrow, Professor of Greek and Greek Literature in Monastery University, a result which none ever regretted.

An earnest throng clustered around the newly-elected president, with hearty congratulations. Not only the trustees, but more than two hundred students, graduates included, who had been nervously waiting outside to hear the news - rushed impetuously as far as they could into the board room, and seizing McLaren, hoisted him to the shoulders of four sturdy men, and then marched out from the chapel into the park singing boisterously their latest college song:

Rah! Rah! Monastery,
Biggest Lion of them all,
Albertson and Mack and Quintin,
Rah! Rah! Rah!

A full moon made it almost as light as day, and even dignified Albertson joined in the jovial song, while Billy Sparrow, dressed in his best blue broadcloth with its bright brass buttons, joined lustily in the chorus: "Rah! Rah! Rah! Albertson, Mack, and Jerry Quintin."

Quintin's team stood at the gate, and its owner told the driver to drive to the farmhouse and wait there. Quintin himself was somewhat nervous, knowing that he had something more to accomplish before he slept.

The leader in this carnival of pleasure and song was Joe Elliot, a next year's senior. He was a stalwart man, the largest in the crowd, six feet four inches in height, broad-shouldered and clear-eyed - a leader in everything he undertook. He stalked in front, bearing a United States flag, setting the pace in both step and song.

Quintin after some effort succeeded in reaching Joe's side, and said to the leader: "Joe, get to the farm as soon as you can and set him down, I want to speak to him as soon as possible. Stop with three cheers for Mack." Joe took the hint, and with march and song, he halted his men in front of the farmhouse, and setting McLaren down, took off his cap, an example which was immediately followed, and they gave three tremendous cheers for the new president of the Monastery and dispersed.

Immediately, grasping McLaren's arm, Quintin said: "We must find Tom and learn whether he has cabled to London." They entered the house and found Nancy at once, as if she had been awaiting their coming, who, without being asked, remarked: "Tom waited until the president was elected, and then started to Centerville, taking Leon with him to cable to London his acceptance. It is about half an hour since they started."

"How did he go?" asked Quintin.

"On foot; he took the boy with him for company. It is such a beautiful night, and the lad wanted to go."

"That is enough," exclaimed Quintin. "Jump in, we may catch him yet. Now, Cyrus, let them go," and they did go. In ten minutes they were in front of the telegraph office at the wharf at Centerville Landing. Just as they began to ascend the stairs a man and a boy came out of the office - Tom and Leonidas.

"Tom, what have you done?" exclaimed McLaren.

"I have just sent my acceptance to London," and, thinking that perhaps he had done wrong in bringing the boy, added, "and it was such a beautiful night, I brought Leon for company."

"But, Tom, why were you so hasty in the matter? Why did you not consult your friends?"

In the meantime Quintin pushed past them into the office, where Reid, the operator, sat.

"Reid," asked Quintin, "have you sent Dr. Sparrow's message?"

"No, sir," was the prompt reply, "but two minutes more and it would have been on the wires; here it is," holding up the yellow paper.

"Hold on, then. It must not go in its present shape."

Reid at once laid the message down on his desk, and turned to other work, feeling assured that it was all right if Quintin and McLaren were interrupting its transit. In the meanwhile McLaren had pushed Tom into a small private room adjoining, and the younger man heard for the first time that he had been elected to the chair of Greek at the Monastery. Then heavy steps were heard and Billy Sparrow rushed into the room exclaiming: "Tom, what have you done?"

"Father," said the young man, "I did what I thought was best. They kindly offered me an honorable place at Burrough Road, and I had no expectation of anything of the kind here, and really did not think that anyone would object, so I accepted; that is all there is to it. I am truly sorry if you don't like what I have done. Had I known it, I might not have been so quick in replying. *But it is now too late*, and we must make the best of it.

But you must remember my future wife is in England."

"No! No!" interrupted Quintin, "It is not too late," and he held up the unsent message. "It has not been sent. Here it is, and your acceptance would be the most unnatural and ungrateful thing you could do. Here is your father and mother. Here is one, who has been to you more than a brother, and here is the fostermother that has fitted you for your great career, and now offers you one of her most important professorships. We are all aware that the girl who is to be your future wife is in England, but think you that Eleen would urge you because of that to make the sacrifice that your acceptance of the Burrough Road professorship demands? No. She would say: 'We are young. We can wait. Stay with your father and mother a while - it will be best.'"

Tom was visibly affected, and after a moment's silence he turned to McLaren. "Carl," he said, "take the blank and fill it out as you think best. You can sign my name," and taking Leon by the hand, together they went out, descended the stairs, and started homeward.

Without a word, McLaren took the blank and wrote: "Honor appreciated, but cannot accept. T. Sparrow, Professor of Greek, Monastery University."

Thus ended a most eventful day at the Monastery.

Quintin was not to be seen. His work for the day was ended when Tom told McLaren to fill out the cablegram; he had slipped away and by this time was in his bed, but not before he had told Cyrus to take the party back to the farm.

Choose from Thousands of 1stWorldLibrary Classics By

A. M. Barnard
Ada Leverson
Adolphus William Ward
Aesop
Agatha Christie
Alexander Aaronsohn
Alexander Kielland
Alexandre Dumas
Alfred Gatty
Alfred Ollivant
Alice Duer Miller
Alice Turner Curtis
Alice Dunbar
Allen Chapman
Ambrose Bierce
Amelia E. Barr
Amory H. Bradford
Andrew Lang
Andrew McFarland Davis
Andy Adams
Anna Alice Chapin
Anna Sewell
Annie Besant
Annie Hamilton Donnell
Annie Payson Call
Annie Roe Carr
Annonaymous
Anton Chekhov
Arnold Bennett
Arthur Conan Doyle
Arthur M. Winfield
Arthur Ransome
Arthur Schnitzler
Atticus
B.H. Baden-Powell
B. M. Bower
B. C. Chatterjee
Baroness Emmuska Orczy
Baroness Orczy
Basil King
Bayard Taylor
Ben Macomber
Bertha Muzzy Bower
Bjornstjerne Bjornson
Booth Tarkington
Boyd Cable
Bram Stoker
C. Collodi
C. E. Orr

C. M. Ingleby
Carolyn Wells
Catherine Parr Traill
Charles A. Eastman
Charles Amory Beach
Charles Dickens
Charles Dudley Warner
Charles Farrar Browne
Charles Ives
Charles Kingsley
Charles Klein
Charles Hanson Towne
Charles Lathrop Pack
Charles Romyn Dake
Charles Whibley
Charles Willing Beale
Charlotte M. Braeme
Charlotte M. Yonge
Charlotte Perkins Stetson
Clair W. Hayes
Clarence Day Jr.
Clarence E. Mulford
Clemence Housman
Confucius
Coningsby Dawson
Cornelis DeWitt Wilcox
Cyril Burleigh
D. H. Lawrence
Daniel Defoe
David Garnett
Dinah Craik
Don Carlos Janes
Donald Keyhoe
Dorothy Kilner
Dougan Clark
Douglas Fairbanks
E. Nesbit
E.P.Roe
E. Phillips Oppenheim
Earl Barnes
Edgar Rice Burroughs
Edith Van Dyne
Edith Wharton
Edward Everett Hale
Edward J. O'Biren
Edward S. Ellis
Edwin L. Arnold
Eleanor Atkins
Eliot Gregory

Elizabeth Gaskell
Elizabeth McCracken
Elizabeth Von Arnim
Ellem Key
Emerson Hough
Emilie F. Carlen
Emily Dickinson
Enid Bagnold
Enilor Macartney Lane
Erasmus W. Jones
Ernie Howard Pie
Ethel May Dell
Ethel Turner
Ethel Watts Mumford
Eugenie Foa
Eugene Wood
Eustace Hale Ball
Evelyn Everett-green
Everard Cotes
F. H. Cheley
F. J. Cross
F. Marion Crawford
Federick Austin Ogg
Ferdinand Ossendowski
Francis Bacon
Francis Darwin
Frances Hodgson Burnett
Frances Parkinson Keyes
Frank Gee Patchin
Frank Harris
Frank Jewett Mather
Frank L. Packard
Frank V. Webster
Frederic Stewart Isham
Frederick Trevor Hill
Frederick Winslow Taylor
Friedrich Kerst
Friedrich Nietzsche
Fyodor Dostoyevsky
G.A. Henty
G.K. Chesterton
Gabrielle E. Jackson
Garrett P. Serviss
Gaston Leroux
George A. Warren
George Ade
Geroge Bernard Shaw
George Durston
George Ebers

George Eliot	Herbert Carter	John Habberton
George Gissing	Herbert N. Casson	John Joy Bell
George MacDonald	Herman Hesse	John Kendrick Bangs
George Meredith	Hildegard G. Frey	John Milton
George Orwell	Homer	John Philip Sousa
George Sylvester Viereck	Honore De Balzac	Jonas Lauritz Idemil Lie
George Tucker	Horace B. Day	Jonathan Swift
George W. Cable	Horace Walpole	Joseph A. Altsheler
George Wharton James	Horatio Alger Jr.	Joseph Carey
Gertrude Atherton	Howard Pyle	Joseph Conrad
Gordon Casserly	Howard R. Garis	Joseph E. Badger Jr
Grace E. King	Hugh Lofting	Joseph Hergesheimer
Grace Gallatin	Hugh Walpole	Joseph Jacobs
Grace Greenwood	Humphry Ward	Jules Vernes
Grant Allen	Ian Maclaren	Julian Hawthrone
Guillermo A. Sherwell	Inez Haynes Gillmore	Julie A Lippmann
Gulielma Zollinger	Irving Bacheller	Justin Huntly McCarthy
Gustav Flaubert	Isabel Hornibrook	Kakuzo Okakura
H. A. Cody	Israel Abrahams	Kenneth Grahame
H. B. Irving	Ivan Turgenev	Kenneth McGaffey
H.C. Bailey	J.G.Austin	Kate Langley Bosher
H. G. Wells	J. Henri Fabre	Kate Langley Bosher
H. H. Munro	J. M. Barrie	Katherine Cecil Thurston
H. Irving Hancock	J. Macdonald Oxley	Katherine Stokes
H. Rider Haggard	J. S. Fletcher	L. A. Abbot
H. W. C. Davis	J. S. Knowles	L. T. Meade
Haldeman Julius	J. Storer Clouston	L. Frank Baum
Hall Caine	Jack London	Latta Griswold
Hamilton Wright Mabie	Jacob Abbott	Laura Dent Crane
Hans Christian Andersen	James Allen	Laura Lee Hope
Harold Avery	James Andrews	Laurence Housman
Harold McGrath	James Baldwin	Lawrence Beasley
Harriet Beecher Stowe	James Branch Cabell	Leo Tolstoy
Harry Castlemon	James DeMille	Leonid Andreyev
Harry Coghill	James Joyce	Lewis Carroll
Harry Houidini	James Lane Allen	Lewis Sperry Chafer
Hayden Carruth	James Lane Allen	Lilian Bell
Helent Hunt Jackson	James Oliver Curwood	Lloyd Osbourne
Helen Nicolay	James Oppenheim	Louis Hughes
Hendrik Conscience	James Otis	Louis Tracy
Hendy David Thoreau	James R. Driscoll	Louisa May Alcott
Henri Barbusse	Jane Austen	Lucy Fitch Perkins
Henrik Ibsen	Jane L. Stewart	Lucy Maud Montgomery
Henry Adams	Janet Aldridge	Luther Benson
Henry Ford	Jens Peter Jacobsen	Lydia Miller Middleton
Henry Frost	Jerome K. Jerome	Lyndon Orr
Henry James	John Burroughs	M. Corvus
Henry Jones Ford	John Cournos	M. H. Adams
Henry Seton Merriman	John F. Kennedy	Margaret E. Sangster
Henry W Longfellow	John Gay	Margret Howth
Herbert A. Giles	John Glasworthy	Margaret Vandercook

Margret Penrose
Maria Edgeworth
Maria Thompson Daviess
Mariano Azuela
Marion Polk Angellotti
Mark Overton
Mark Twain
Mary Austin
Mary Catherine Crowley
Mary Cole
Mary Hastings Bradley
Mary Roberts Rinehart
Mary Rowlandson
M. Wollstonecraft Shelley
Maud Lindsay
Max Beerbohm
Myra Kelly
Nathaniel Hawthrone
Nicolo Machiavelli
O. F. Walton
Oscar Wilde
Owen Johnson
P.G. Wodehouse
Paul and Mabel Thorne
Paul G. Tomlinson
Paul Severing
Percy Brebner
Peter B. Kyne
Plato
R. Derby Holmes
R. L. Stevenson
R. S. Ball
Rabindranath Tagore
Rahul Alvares
Ralph Bonehill
Ralph Henry Barbour
Ralph Victor
Ralph Waldo Emmerson
Rene Descartes
Rex Beach

Rex E. Beach
Richard Harding Davis
Richard Jefferies
Richard Le Gallienne
Robert Barr
Robert Frost
Robert Gordon Anderson
Robert L. Drake
Robert Lansing
Robert Lynd
Robert Michael Ballantyne
Robert W. Chambers
Rosa Nouchette Carey
Rudyard Kipling
Samuel B. Allison
Samuel Hopkins Adams
Sarah Bernhardt
Sarah C. Hallowell
Selma Lagerlof
Sherwood Anderson
Sigmund Freud
Standish O'Grady
Stanley Weyman
Stella Benson
Stella M. Francis
Stephen Crane
Stewart Edward White
Stijn Streuvels
Swami Abhedananda
Swami Parmananda
T. S. Ackland
T. S. Arthur
The Princess Der Ling
Thomas A. Janvier
Thomas A Kempis
Thomas Anderton
Thomas Bailey Aldrich
Thomas Bulfinch
Thomas De Quincey
Thomas Dixon

Thomas H. Huxley
Thomas Hardy
Thomas More
Thornton W. Burgess
U. S. Grant
Valentine Williams
Various Authors
Vaughan Kester
Victor Appleton
Victoria Cross
Virginia Woolf
Wadsworth Camp
Walter Camp
Walter Scott
Washington Irving
Wilbur Lawton
Wilkie Collins
Willa Cather
Willard F. Baker
William Dean Howells
William le Queux
W. Makepeace Thackeray
William W. Walter
William Shakespeare
Winston Churchill
Yei Theodora Ozaki
Yogi Ramacharaka
Young E. Allison
Zane Grey